"Mary J. Nelson has done it again . . . written a book that touches the deepest places of my heart. We all go through trials, some more than others . . . and what helps is having a hand to grab in the middle of the fire. Through her book, *Grace for Tough Times,* Mary has offered not only a hand, but a hope that will see all of us through the tough moments. Get a copy, not only for yourself, but for those friends who are doing their best to stay afloat in very stormy seas."

—**Holly Wagner**, Author of *Godchicks; When it Pours, He Reigns; Daily Steps for Godchicks*

"Mary J. Nelson's *Grace for Touch Times* is a wonderful book to show us how to pass life's ten greatest tests and reach spiritual maturity. I recommend it!"

—**Alice Smith**, Executive Director, U.S. Prayer Center

"What a wonderful book! Radiating warmth, its pages spill over with practical wisdom on how to connect with God, receive his grace, and move on with your life when tough times stand between you and your future."

—**Dr. Gary D. Kinnaman**, Author and Senior Pastor, Word of Grace Church

"Mary J. Nelson has come through the Refiner's fire, not once, but many times. She has come to know his voice and trust his promises. *Grace for Tough Times* vividly describes each test you might face in life's journey. Her counsel, the personal stories, and the powerful passages from Scripture will help you 'to drink deeply from the well of his infinite love.' If you are discouraged or frightened, angry or lonely, this book comes just at the right time. You will be refreshed, and hope will be restored."

—**Bill Bohline**, Lead Pastor, Hosanna! Lutheran Church

"In *Grace for Tough Times,* Mary J. Nelson delivers God's message of hope and help for our hurts and brokenness. Her inspiring personal stories provide comfort that as Christians we are not alone when we struggle. The ten tests of the tough times are presented in a clear and concise manner, which will profoundly transform every reader with an open heart and mind."

—**Rose Busscher**, PsyD, LP, Christian Psychologist at Life Development Resources

"From start to finish, Mary J. Nelson has woven real-life thoughts and experiences together in a way that both refreshes and comforts. I believe this book will help change people's hearts and thoughts in areas of life that seem difficult and unchangeable. In dark times, it will ignite peaceful light and renewed hope. A must-read book for all seasons and situations of life."

—**Pat Moe**, Pastor of Care Ministry, Hosanna! Lutheran Church

GRACE

for
TOUGH TIMES
by Mary J. Nelson

KEYS TO HOPE, COMFORT *and* ENCOURAGEMENT

BETHANY HOUSE PUBLISHERS

Minneapolis, Minnesota

Published by Bethany House Publishers
11400 Hampshire Avenue South
Bloomington, Minnesota 55438

Bethany House Publishers is a division of
Baker Publishing Group, Grand Rapids, Michigan.

Printed in the United States of America

ISBN-13:   978-0-7642-0213-1
ISBN-10:   0-7642-0213-8

Library of Congress Cataloging-in-Publication Data

Nelson, Mary J. (Mary Jeanne)
    Grace for tough times: keys to hope, comfort, and encouragement / Mary J.
Nelson.
        p.   cm.
    Summary: "These devotions explore human responses to difficult, painful
experiences. The book provides discussions about the challenges to faith that
inevitably come in times of trial, and true accounts of how God's grace finds those
who continue to seek him"—Provided by publisher.
    ISBN 0-7642-0213-8 (pbk.)
    1. Suffering—Prayer-books and devotions—English. 2. Consolation. I. Title.
    BV4909.N45   2006
    242'.4—dc22   2006013585

TO MY LIFELONG FRIEND

Deb Goodnature

who met God face-to-face in the fire;

TO HER SON

Corey

who gave his life for freedom;

TO OUR LORD AND SAVIOR

Jesus Christ

who gave His life to save us all.

MARY J. NELSON is a speaker and the author of *Grace for Each Hour*, a devotional book for women undergoing breast cancer treatment. A survivor of breast cancer, she disciples and prays for other women who face the disease and leads the Pray for the Cure cancer ministry at Hosanna!, a church of 5,000 members where she also serves on the vision board. Mary has worked in healthcare education and training for more than twenty-five years and is president and founder of Soterion, a healthcare communications consulting firm. She and her husband, Howie, have two adult children and make their home in Lakeville, Minnesota. Avid motorcyclists, Mary and Howie enjoy taking road trips with other enthusiasts and are leaders in Hosanna! Bikers, a ministry that reaches more than 350 fellow bikers.

You may contact Mary at:

maryjnelson@soterion.net.

Acknowledgments

For making this book a reality, my deepest gratitude goes to . . .

My heavenly Father, my King and Provider: for meeting me in the fire and covering me with your grace, and for allowing me to participate in the sacred work of your kingdom. May this book bring you glory as you continue to raise harvesters out of the refining fire.

Howie, my husband, friend, and soul mate: for loving me through this project, for praying us through the tough times, and for listening to my heart. I'll follow you anywhere the Gold Wing will take us.

My son, Bryan: for checking in regularly on my progress with the book, and for believing Mom can do anything.

My daughter, Kelly: for your love, friendship, and late-night conversations, and for being a young woman after God's own heart. You amaze me.

My WPs Mary Carroll, Julie Swecker, and Barb Wilson, and to SOWP Laura Carroll: for sharing my joy and loving the real me, and for your prayers and encouragement as I labored through each test of the fire.

Kalifornia Kids, 5Bs, and Hosanna! Bikers: for keeping me real, and for showing kindness toward others that inspires me to love like Jesus.

My pastors, prayer partners, and friends at Hosanna! in Lakeville, Minnesota: for warming my heart and nourishing my spirit when I return home to the aircraft carrier.

Kyle Duncan, Julie Smith, Jeanne Hedrick, and the entire Bethany House family: for using your creative talents to bring glory to the Father, and for helping me bring hope and encouragement to those who need it most.

My parents, family, and friends: for supporting and encouraging me when the flames burned hottest.

And finally, thanks to the Goodnature family and everyone whose personal journey through the refining fire provided inspiration for the stories and testimonies in this book. May others discover His grace through your tough times.

TABLE OF CONTENTS

But now, O Israel, the Lord who created you says:

"Do not be afraid, for I have ransomed you.

I have called you by name; you are mine.

When you go through deep waters and great trouble,

I will be with you.

When you go through rivers of difficulty, you will not drown!

When you walk through the fire of oppression,

you will not be burned up;

the flames will not consume you."

—ISAIAH 43:1–2

Preface

I've walked through the fires of oppression. The tough times. If you're holding this book, so have you. Maybe you're feeling the heat right now. The fire blazes around you. The roaring flames leap up from the depths of your suffering, threatening to consume you and steal all in this world you call your own. You gasp for each breath, the smoke stinging your eyes and searing your throat. The heat intensifies as you battle to keep the flames from destroying your hopes and dreams. As your foundation begins to crumble beneath, you try frantically to escape with your life in one piece.

If today you find yourself in the furnace of suffering, take heart. You don't have to burn. You can walk away untouched by the flames. But you will never again be the same person who entered the blazing inferno. I know. I've been there. For five years the fire raged. Just when the embers began to die down, it seemed as though someone stoked the fire, or worse, threw a little gasoline on the coals.

It all started when a tree fell into my living room during a terrible spring windstorm. Cleanup and $30,000 worth of home repairs carried us well into the fall. Then, one week into our hopes for a more promising new year, my husband lost his job.

Several months passed in the furnace of suffering. He was barely employed again, thankfully with full health benefits, when I was diagnosed with breast cancer. The fire raged on. Chemo, radiation, wigs, and more trips to the doctor than I care to count consumed the remainder of that year and most of the next.

When it was finally over, I peeked out of the furnace into a bright beautiful winter day one week into the New Year with high hopes. I didn't see the icy patch until it was too late. The flames roared again. Two years of physical therapy and one knee surgery later, we were certain the coals had turned to ashes. We didn't see the hot embers smoldering underneath. Again, it was the first week into the New Year. They were sorry, but due to the post–9/11 business slump, they had to terminate my husband's job. And again, the fire roared. Another fourteen months passed in the furnace of suffering before he found employment.

The fire of oppression will either cause you to burn up or help you grow stronger. If you choose to walk through the fire on your own strength, the flames will consume you. But if you invite the Lord into the middle of the fire, He will protect you. The flames won't touch you. After all, you belong to Him. He has ransomed you and called you by name.

This book is filled with testimonies and promises of God's amazing love, how He carried others through the fire, and how He can carry you. If you turn to Him, He'll give you all the hope, comfort, and encouragement you need to endure the intense heat. He'll give you grace for tough times.

Tests of the Fire

These trials are only to test your faith, to show that it is

strong and pure. It is being tested as fire tests and purifies gold—

and your faith is far more precious to God than mere gold.

So if your faith remains strong after being tried by fiery trials,

it will bring you much praise and glory and honor on the day

when Jesus Christ is revealed to the whole world.

—1 Peter 1:7

What was your life like before the fire? I can imagine it was a lot like mine. I can see you resting comfortably on a four-legged stool. Each leg represents your human support and material help—the first, your possessions and financial security, and the second, your health. The third leg is your relationships, and the fourth, your strength and abilities. Suddenly, a leg falls out from under the stool. You lose your job or your business. You face a life-threatening disease or a debilitating accident. You experience devastating personal failure. Your marriage breaks up, your home is destroyed, or you lose a loved one. The stool crumbles beneath you. Another leg falls. And another.

But why, Lord? Why would a loving God allow such terrible things to happen to me? Because we live in a fallen world. Tough times can come from the sin of others or even from our own sin. Sometimes it's an attack from Satan. Sometimes it comes to prepare us for special service. Sometimes, we simply don't know. We *do* know that suffering brings us face-to-face with the most important question we will ever encounter: Is our faith real or isn't it? Are we Christ followers or aren't we? We will never know for sure until we've been "battle-tested."

Jesus said if our faith has shallow roots or we have no faith at all, the hot winds of testing will blow us over (Luke 8:13). But if our roots penetrate deeply into the soil of His love, we can stand tall through the winds of testing and reap a huge harvest of blessing.

How deep are your roots? You won't know until testing comes. And it *will* come. It came to Eve in the Garden of Eden. It came to the Israelites in the desert. It came to Jesus in the wilderness. It came to Peter the night Jesus was crucified. Sooner or later, it will come to you too. Jesus said we would have many trials and sorrows on this earth (John 16:33). When the legs fall out from under your stool, your soul is laid bare. Your character is exposed. The testing that follows can teach perseverance and strengthen your endurance, so you're better prepared for the next time the stool crumbles (James 1:2–4).

If your fire is *really* intense, take heart. Big assignments require big character. Moses was alone in the desert for forty years before God called him to rescue the Israelites from Egypt. Paul spent three years in Arabia after his call to ministry on the road to Damascus. David was anointed king but spent many years hiding in caves and running for his life from King Saul. Joseph was sold into slavery by his own brothers and imprisoned for thirteen years before he became ruler of Egypt and saved the nation of Israel from starvation.

All these heroes of faith faced a time of separation between their old lives and the new. Each experienced persecution, disloyalty, and hardship. But God used the tough times to gain their undivided attention. With all their comforts removed, they could hear His voice, experience His love, and trust His provision in brand-new ways. Through this time of character-building, He removed the impurities that hindered their relationship with Him. He refined them in the furnace of suffering (Isaiah 48:10). Then He sent them out to bring about His good purposes (Romans 8:28).

Yes, our God sits as a refiner and purifier of silver (Malachi 3:3). He is like the silversmith in the refining process, and we are like raw metal. The silversmith heats the raw metal in the middle of the fire where the flames are the hottest, until the silver melts and the impurities rise to the surface. Then he skims the impurities off the top, leaving pure metal. Throughout the process of heating and melting, he never leaves the silver unattended. If he leaves it in the fire a moment too long, the silver is destroyed. Finally, when his reflection appears in the clear pure surface of the silver, the silversmith knows the process is complete.

Ministering to others facing tough times, I've discovered we all face certain tests in the refining fire, even though our circumstances may differ. As we struggle through these tests, the impurities slowly burn away, leaving a little bit more of the Silversmith's reflection and a deeper understanding of the nature of God.

You will always have a choice as you face the tests of the fire. If you yield to God, the tough times can be a season of growth (Daniel 12:10). When you lean on His strength to endure the heat, He draws you close to His heart and reveals the secret treasures buried within each test. When Joseph was a slave in Egypt, his positive response to each new setback and his total dependence on God resulted in strong character and deep wisdom (Genesis 37, 39–47). Like Joseph, the refining fire can become an opportunity for God to transform you into the person He created you to be (Romans 5:3). It can take you to a place of complete trust in His nature, whatever might happen (Job 13:15). As silver in the refining process, you are cleansed, purified, and available to participate in the sacred work of His kingdom (2 Timothy 2:21).

You can also let the refining fire become a furnace of destruction. Judas and King Saul let each fiery test push them further away from God. When the Jewish high council decided to kill Jesus, and it became clear He would not rule an earthly kingdom, Judas betrayed Him, hung himself, and went to his grave filled with sorrow (Matthew 27:3–5). Peter, in denying that he knew Him, betrayed Jesus too; but the refining fire brought him broken and remorseful to the feet of Christ (John 21:15–17).

Saul was anointed king of Israel, but as he faced difficult tests of leadership, his jealousy, disobedience, and need for control eventually cost him the throne. David also faced persecution after God anointed him king, but he yielded to God and let his character be refined. In the Psalms, he cries out from a deep level of suffering while singing praises to God for His unfailing love. Judas and Saul flunked the tests of the fire. Peter and David passed with flying colors.

How will you respond to the tough times? Will you miss God in the fire or will you invite Him into the center? When all the legs on your stool of life are gone, and nothing remains but Jesus, will you discover He's all you need? If you seek Him in the furnace of suffering, you will never regret your decision. In the middle of the fire, where the flames burn hottest, you meet the Almighty God face-to-face. You drink from the well of His infinite love.

Instead of resenting Him through the tough times, you finally realize that it is only by His grace that you live and move (Acts 17:28). You discover that a single day in His presence is better than a thousand anywhere else (Psalm 84:10). Like Jacob, who set up a stone pillar at Bethel to remember the place where he wrestled with God, you will never forget the sacred place where God met you in the fire (Genesis 35:14).

If you're ready to meet God in the tough times, this book is for you. It will guide you on a spiritual journey through ten tests you may encounter in the refining fire. As you read the devotions within each test, God's grace will soak like a soothing balm into the heat of your pain. In each reading, you will find comforting Scripture, stories of hope, words of encouragement, and a prayer to help you yield to God and break through the barriers that can keep you from deeper intimacy with Jesus. You might choose to devote one week for each test and read one devotion each weekday for a ten-week personal study.

Like any good and faithful teacher, the Lord wants to see you pass each test. Jesus knew Peter would deny Him, but He prayed for Peter to pass the test of faith (Luke 22:31–32). And He was grieved when the Israelites failed their test (1 Corinthians 10:5). Today, as you battle the flames that threaten to destroy your hopes and dreams, your Teacher is praying for you, and all the angels of heaven are clapping and cheering you on. And He has wonderful news—it's an open-book test! The answers to every struggle you face are as close as your Bible. Keep it handy as you read each devotion. You will find a key verse at the beginning and several Bible references woven throughout the text for further study. I recommend a good study Bible in either the New Living Translation (NLT) or the New International Version (NIV). Don't despair if you fall short. God will never give up on you. His tender mercies start fresh every day (Lamentations 3:23).

So come as you are. Let the Silversmith refine you. Start by inviting Him into your fire. Let Him cleanse and purify you so the power and glory of God can flow through you (Hebrews 12:1–2). Don't worry. He won't let you burn. He'll give you strength to endure the intense heat. His grace will comfort and encourage your soul. As He holds you close to His heart, He'll gently remove all the impurities until you're strong in character and ready for anything (James 1:2–4). When your fiery trials are over, it will bring you much praise, glory, and honor on the day when Jesus comes!

Heavenly Father, I need you. I know you love me and have a perfect plan for my life, even during the tough times I am facing today. I know I have fallen short. Thank you for sending your Son to die on the cross for my sins. I receive you as my Lord and Savior. Please come into the middle of my fire. Show me everything you want to teach me. Lord, you are bigger than the fire that rages around me. Please protect me and cover me with your grace. In Jesus' name, amen.

DARE TO BELIEVE

THE FAITH TEST

What is faith? It is the confident assurance that what we hope for is going to happen. It is the evidence of things we cannot yet see.

—HEBREWS 11:1

RECEIVE YOUR REWARD

So, you see, it is impossible to please God without faith. Anyone who wants to come to him must believe that there is a God and that he rewards those who sincerely seek him.

—HEBREWS 11:6

I never saw the cancer. I just believed four doctors who claimed it was there. The first one said it felt like cancer. The second doctor said it looked like cancer on the ultrasound film. Another one surgically removed the offending clump of tissue, and a fourth doctor examined it under a microscope. A fifth doctor believed the claims of the other four. Even though I felt perfectly healthy, I allowed him to infuse my body with eight doses of powerful chemotherapy drugs that temporarily stole my hair, my dignity, and what was left of my perfect health—all to kill the invisible cancer.

I can't see God either, but the apostle Paul tells me I have no excuse whatsoever for not knowing Him. I know the truth about Him instinctively, because God has placed this knowledge in my heart. His handiwork in nature and the heavens shows me a God of intelligence, detail, order, and beauty. He makes clear the invisible qualities of a personally involved Creator who controls all the powerful forces of the universe (Romans 1:19–20; Psalms 19:1–4).

His secret plan all along was to give us direct access to the Creator through His Son, Jesus Christ (Ephesians 1:9). Moved by His passionate love for His creation, the Creator became part of it. He

came to earth in human form and became subject to all human
limitations of time, space, suffering, and death. He knew our sinful
human nature would never allow us to be righteous and holy
enough to come into fellowship with Him by our own efforts. So
He sacrificed himself in our place. When we accept His precious
gift and trust Jesus to take away our sins, we are made right in
God's sight, regardless of our background or past behavior. It is
only by our faith in Christ, not our good deeds, that we are set
free (Romans 3:21–22, 26–27).

This man Jesus is the visible image of the invisible God (Colossians 1:15). Hundreds claimed to have heard His teachings and
witnessed His miracles. The Bible recounts eyewitness testimony
to His life on earth, His sacrifice on the cross, and His triumph
over death. Many miraculous signs were recorded so we would
believe He is the Son of God (John 20:30–31). If all the miracles
He performed were written down, the whole world couldn't con-
tain the books (John 21:25)! It occurred to me in the midst of
chemo treatments, baldness, and wigs that I have more evidence of
my Savior's existence than I ever had of my cancer.

In spite of all the evidence—even after countless miracles and
over three hundred prophecies that came true before their very
eyes—there were doubters. The Jewish leaders cared more about
their political ambitions than leading people to God. They
harassed Jesus for healing on the Sabbath, criticized the company
He kept, accused Him of blasphemy and demon-possession, plotted His murder, and condemned Him to death (John 5:16, 10:20;
Matthew 26:57–68). His own family and the people in his hometown refused to believe in Him (Mark 6:3–6; John 7:3–5). Even
His beloved disciples had their doubts. Judas betrayed Him to the
leading priests (Luke 22:47–48). Peter denied knowing Him three
times after His arrest (Luke 22:54–62). Thomas doubted, even
after all the other disciples told him they had seen the risen Christ.
He refused to believe unless he could see for himself and put his

finger in the nail holes in Jesus' hands (John 20:24–25). Eight days later, when Jesus appeared to them again, He gave Thomas his proof. Then He made a profound statement about the importance of faith. He said to Thomas, "You believe because you have seen me. Blessed are those who haven't seen me and believe anyway" (John 20:29).

Do you dare to believe? There are still scoffers today—like Jodi's mom—who try to help you by denying the existence of God. Two abusive husbands, ongoing financial struggles, and four children whose lives were riddled with addiction, depression, mental illness, and tragedy left her with a hardened heart toward anything of God. But Jodi wanted more. A friend introduced her to Jesus when her own marriage broke up, her life was in shambles, and she had nowhere else to turn. And Jesus transformed her life.

He brought her into fellowship with Christian friends who loved her and cared and prayed for her. He restored her marriage and her hope. He broke the cycle of poverty, bitterness, fear, and addiction. He healed her body and her soul. Yet when she shared the reason for her hope, Jodi's mom laughed and said believing in God was like believing in Santa Claus. Jodi never knew Santa; he never visited her house as a child. But she knew Jesus. She knew He was real. And she knew a real miracle when she saw one.

Is He real to you? Sometimes you might wonder. There are times in the fire when all you hear is an eerie silence. You cry out to God for help, but your prayers seem to evaporate into the flames. The next time you feel trapped and alone, take a peek outside the furnace of suffering. Watch a glorious sunrise or gaze up at the millions of stars He placed in the sky. Let the awesome majesty of His creation remind you that He still sits on the throne, controlling the powerful forces of heaven and earth. After all, He hid this knowledge in your heart.

But believing He exists is only the beginning. Over 80 percent of the population acknowledges that much. Even Satan believes in God (James 2:19). He wants more from you. He wants a real and personal relationship with you that will transform your life forever. Dare to believe it! Come to Him in faith and receive your reward.

Heavenly Father, forgive me for my unbelief. Forgive me for doubting your power, your purposes, and your faithfulness. Thank you for the detail, order, and beauty of your creation and for hiding this knowledge of you deep in my heart. I believe in you, Lord! But I want to know you as more than my God and Creator. I want to know you as my Savior and friend. Please strengthen my faith and increase my desire for you. I want more of you, Lord! I want to tell of your miracles. Help me to seek you with all my heart and soul. In Jesus' name, amen.

HE'S ON YOUR SIDE

If God is for us, who can ever be against us? Since God did not spare even his own Son but gave him up for us all, won't God, who gave us Christ, also give us everything else?

—ROMANS 8:31–32

She hadn't set foot in a church since confirmation class. She cowered in the back of the prayer chapel with tears in her eyes, paralyzed in fear of the cancer diagnosis she had received the day before. *But you don't understand. I've ignored God all my life. Why should He help me now? I feel guilty even asking.*

They were the parents of a hero. As a nation mourned their loss, their strong faith carried them through the shock and grief of losing a son to enemy fire during combat operations. But sometimes the intensity of their pain gave way to doubt. *We assumed he would be safe. We should have prayed more.*

She spent her last days in hospice care. Slowly and painfully, the cancer ravaged whatever life remained in her weak and withering forty-year-old body. Her family begged her to allow a pastor to come and visit. *God didn't care about me when I was healthy. Why should He care about me now?*

In the heat of the fire, it can be tempting to doubt the nature of God. It can be tempting to think He's given up on us, He's punishing us, or He simply doesn't care. But the God I know doesn't condemn, steal, kill, or destroy. There is a thief prowling around among us who handles all those functions quite well, and his name is Satan. No, my God's purpose is to give life in all its fullness (John 10:10). There is no condemnation in Him (Romans 8:1). His love for me knows no boundaries (Hosea 14:4). He delights in me (Psalm 18:19). His greatest joy is when I want nothing more than to sit in His presence and fellowship with Him. He has compassion for the sick and the hurting (Matthew 14:14) and weeps along with us when a loved one is lost (John 11:34–36).

Yes, our God is filled with grace and mercy. And *you* are His precious masterpiece (Ephesians 2:10). You are perfectly and wonderfully made, and His thoughts about you far outnumber the grains of sand on the beach (Psalm 139:14, 17–18). His love is big enough to reach every corner of your life. It's wide enough to cover the sorrows of today and long enough to cover your uncertain tomorrows. It reaches the heights of your good times and the depths of your despair (Ephesians 3:17–19). There is nothing—not disaster, unemployment, financial ruin, broken relationships, sickness, or even death—that can ever keep His love away from you (Romans 8:38).

And if you've been away for a while, don't think for one minute your God has given up on you. He is happier for the one sheep who wanders away from the flock and is found than for the ninety-nine righteous sheep who are back home safe in the sheepfold (Luke 15:4–7). Just as a woman with ten valuable coins searches high and low for the one she lost and rejoices when she finds it, there is joy in the presence of God's angels when even one person repents and turns back to God (Luke 15:8–10). Jesus tells of the lost son who returned home hungry and broke after squandering his inheritance on prostitutes and wild living. His father welcomed him with open arms and threw a party in his honor (Luke

15:11–32). So it is with your heavenly Father. You are His precious child and He never stops pursuing you. He grieves when you are lost and rejoices with all the angels in heaven when you come back home to Him.

In your fire today, you may doubt His grace, mercy, and love. If you are tempted to wonder if your God has switched sides and is collaborating with the enemy, let me ask you a question: Would you strike your own children with a devastating disease or tragedy, and then abandon them in the middle of nowhere as a punishment for their misbehavior? If your children asked you for a loaf of bread, would you give them a stone? If they asked you for a fish, would you give them a snake? I didn't think so. Jesus said if we sinful and fallible people know how to give good gifts to our children, then how much more will our heavenly Father give them to us (Matthew 7:9–11).

Your God is not vindictive, indifferent, or selfish. He is a loving Father who understands and cares for you, infinitely more so than the best earthly parent. He loves you so much that He didn't even spare His own Son—He gave Him up just for you. And won't God, who gave you Christ, give you everything else you need? Of course He will. He's on your side. And if He's with you, who or what can ever stand against you?

Heavenly Father, forgive me for doubting you and your love for me. Forgive me for wandering away from you and blaming you for the pain and suffering in my life. I am amazed by your grace and mercy, and I want to come home. I want nothing more than to sit in your awesome presence and soak in your unconditional love. Thank you for being a compassionate Father who never gives up on me, who delights in my every thought, understands my situation, and cares deeply about my pain. I know you only want the best for me. Thank you for being on my side. In Jesus' name, amen.

BELIEVE HE CAN

I am the Lord, the God of all the peoples of the world.

Is anything too hard for me?

—JEREMIAH 32:27

My life is full of miracles. I came into the world breech, a medical term for hind-side first. A difficult forceps delivery left the doctor amazed there was no permanent damage to my delicate little body. My own son was born with a true knot in his umbilical cord. Again, the doctor was amazed, since such babies are often stillborn or oxygen deprived. Mine was perfectly healthy. Later, doctors diagnosed a life-threatening tubal pregnancy in the nick of time, before it ruptured. A second tubal pregnancy left me unable to have any more children, but not before the birth of my second child, a beautiful baby girl. Interesting . . . a heart defect discovered while I was pregnant miraculously disappeared after her birth. And then . . . miracle of miracles! The Lord reached down into a bald and dark place called cancer and changed my life forever. He healed my body and won my soul. *Oh Lord, you have done so many miracles for me! If I tried to list them all, I would never come to the end* (Psalm 40:5).

So why, two years later, did I sit in a pile on the floor, convinced that my husband would never work again and we were destined for the poorhouse? Why, after the sixth promising opportunity fell through, did I doubt God was capable of overcoming my husband's age, the sluggish 9/11 economy, high unemployment, and his shrinking industry?

I'm not the first believer to watch God perform miracle after miracle, only to wonder if He's up to the task *this* time. The Israelites wandered the desert for forty years because they didn't believe God could muster up enough power to finish what He started. He had heard their cries for help and sent His servant Moses and ten plagues to rescue them from four hundred years of slavery in Egypt (Exodus 7:14–12:42). With the Pharaoh in hot pursuit, Moses simply raised his hands and God parted the water of the Red Sea, allowing the people to cross over on dry land. When they had all crossed, Moses repeated the gesture, causing the roaring waters to rise again, killing the entire army of Pharaoh (Exodus 14:15–31).

When they were thirsty in the desert, He made bitter water suitable for drinking and fresh water come from a rock (Exodus 15:22–25, 17:5–6). Every day they ate the manna He sent from heaven (Exodus 16:1–36). When they wanted meat, He sent them more quail than they could eat (Numbers 11:31). He sent a pillar of cloud by day and a pillar of fire by night to guide them in their travels (Numbers 9:15–22). Yet in spite of being eyewitnesses to all these miraculous signs and wonders, they refused to enter the land God promised to give them (Numbers 14:1–4). They wouldn't believe He could defeat the powerful giants and overcome their fortified cities.

Even the disciples doubted. Immediately after watching Jesus feed five thousand people with five loaves of bread and two fish, they boarded a boat while Jesus went to the hills to pray. In the middle of the night a storm raged, and they were in serious danger. When Jesus came to them by walking on the water, they screamed in terror. He immediately calmed the storm, but He was astonished that they still couldn't believe He could rescue them, even after witnessing the miracle of the fishes and loaves (Mark 6:45–52).

Maybe you can relate to the Israelites wandering the desert or the disciples fighting for their lives in the midst of the storm. You watch His miracles. You believe nothing is impossible for Him. But in the heat of the fire, you doubt. You can't imagine you'll ever work again. You're convinced God can't heal your marriage, your illness, or your broken heart.

You desperately want to believe. *Lord, help me not to doubt!* You cry out to Jesus, just like the father who sought healing for his deaf and mute son. He cried out to Jesus: "Have mercy on us and help us. Do something if you can." "What do you mean, 'If I can'?" Jesus asked. "Anything is possible if a person believes." The father instantly replied, "I do believe, but help me not to doubt!" (Mark 9:22–24). Jesus responded by healing his son. He knew how desperately the father *wanted* to believe. And He knows how desperately *you* want to believe too.

Jesus didn't condemn this father for doubting, and He won't condemn you. Just a tiny amount of faith in the power of God is enough to move your mountain. Jesus said if you had faith as small as a mustard seed, nothing would be impossible (Matthew 17:20). Faith is not something we obtain on our own power. Like salvation, it is a gift from God (Ephesians 2:8–9). Don't worry that your faith feels small and your doubt feels big. There is great power in just a little faith when you believe in God's power to act. And anything is possible if you believe, because nothing is impossible for God.

The Israelites were a stubborn people. Doubt and unbelief in the power of God kept all but two from entering the Promised Land (Numbers 14:20–30). The disciples worked side-by-side with Jesus, but they too were a little slow to catch on (Matthew 8:17–18). So are we sometimes. We doubt, even though the pages of our Bible are filled with the testimonies of believers who walked alongside Him and witnessed His power. We doubt, even though the Holy Spirit dwelling inside of us is our direct hot line to the heavenly Father. We doubt, even though our lives are filled with miracles. When the flames of your fire burn hot today—when you're wondering if God is up to the task *this* time—remember what Christ has done for you and have faith He will do it again. Nothing is too hard when you believe He can!

Heavenly Father, forgive me for doubting your power to rescue me. Thank you for the miracles in my life and all you have done for me. If I tried to list all your blessings and miracles, I would never come to the end! Lord, I especially thank you for the gift of faith. I know I only need a tiny amount of faith in your power to move my mountain. So please, Lord, give me more. Please increase and strengthen my faith. I believe you can, Lord! I believe nothing is too hard for you. Please help me not to doubt! In Jesus' name, amen.

BELIEVE HE WILL

Without wavering, let us hold tightly to the hope we say we have,

for God can be trusted to keep his promise.

—HEBREWS 10:23

We pray backwards. We lift our praises, confessions, and requests up to God, and then we wait for the answers to be manifest in the material realm. We believe His promise that everyone who asks will receive (Matthew 7:8). If the answers don't come the way we expect, we doubt He hears, we doubt He cares, or we doubt He exists at all.

But if the Lord comes through with a really big answer to a really big prayer, we're often so surprised and amazed that we shout it from the rooftops. *Look what the Lord did! He healed me! Can you believe it?* In most cases, we receive, and *then* we believe, but the Lord expects us to believe first, and *then* receive (Matthew 21:22). He said we need to become as little children (Matthew 18:3). And most little children aren't jumping up and down, surprised and amazed at their parents' faithfulness. *Look what my mom did! She fed me today. Can you believe it?*

No, children need little more than kindness and a gentle touch to have faith in the adults who care for them. Their faith is pure and simple. They haven't yet experienced the visible inconsistencies and religious traditions that cast doubt on the beliefs of many adults. When children pray, they simply believe that God will answer. They won't point out ten examples of when He didn't.

When children are taught about the miracles in the Bible, they simply believe them. As adults, we can't help wondering sometimes if biblical miracles are really just stories, and modern-day miracles are really coincidences. We try to make sense out of the world we live in, so we often pull God down to our level of human understanding. Children don't need to understand all the mysteries of God's kingdom and solve all the apparent impossibilities in the material realm in order to have faith. They simply believe and expect to receive.

The Bible is filled with stories of people with childlike faith—people who asked for God's favor, believed in His promises, and expected to receive them. People like Noah, who built a huge boat in the middle of dry land to save his family from the flood that destroyed the rest of mankind (Hebrews 11:7). People like Moses, who forfeited his comfortable position as the Pharaoh's adopted grandson to lead a million of his own people out of slavery in Egypt (Hebrews 11:24–27). People like Gideon, Samson, David, Samuel, and all the prophets, who overthrew kingdoms, governed with justice, shut the mouths of lions, and defeated the mightiest armies (Hebrews 11:32–35). People like the Roman officer who believed Jesus needed only to speak the command from a distance and his servant would be healed (Luke 7:1–8). People like the woman who believed her hemorrhaging would stop if only she touched the edge of Jesus' robe (Mark 5:25–29).

People like Abraham. Imagine the faith it took for a childless old man to believe God's promise to give him a son who would make his descendents as numerous as the stars (Genesis 15:4–5). Several years later, when he was ninety-nine years old and his wife, Sarah, was almost as old, God promised again to make him the father of many nations. He even changed his name from Abram to Abraham, which meant "father of many" (Genesis 17:4–5).

Abraham never doubted that God would keep His promise. He

was absolutely convinced that God would do what He said He would do (Romans 4:20–21). Every time Abraham used his new name, he spoke God's promise in faith over his current circumstances. He called himself the father of many for years before it was manifest. And when he was one hundred years old, God honored his faithfulness. Much to Sarah's delight, she bore her husband a son at the ripe old age of ninety (Genesis 21:1–7). God's promise to give them millions of descendents was fulfilled through Jesus Christ, who came from Abraham's line.

Imagine having faith like Abraham—faith that isn't moved by the hopelessness of your current circumstances, faith like a child's that simply believes and expects to receive. Jennifer had that kind of faith. When she married Mark, they both enjoyed the late nights and wild parties. Jennifer settled down after the kids were born, but Mark kept right on partying with his friends. Weekend softball games, football parties, sporting events, and fishing trips often led to long nights of barhopping, after-hours drinking, and recreational drug use.

Jennifer lived like a single parent on weekends. She felt emotionally abandoned, and her complaints fell on deaf ears. She was on the verge of leaving Mark when a neighbor invited her and the kids to a playgroup at her church, and her life began to change. Jennifer joined the church, started attending a Bible study, and began meeting weekly with a group of Christian moms. Then she started praying.

With members of her small group she prayed for Mark every day. Every Sunday morning she would get the kids ready for church and invite Mark to join them. And every Sunday morning he refused. She never argued. She continued to invite him, fully expecting that some day he would get up and go with her. One morning, he did. An old friend had invited him to a Christian men's conference the day before, and God stirred something in his heart. God answered Jennifer's prayers and then some. He not only restored her marriage and saved her husband, but also lifted him into a spiritual leadership role. Mark eventually became a pastor.

Today, imagine you have faith like Abraham's and the great faith heroes of the Bible. Imagine your faith is like a child's. As a child trusts a loving parent, you come before your heavenly Father with a humble and sincere heart, weak and dependent on Him for your every need. You are fully convinced He will answer your prayers. You believe it's His will to rescue you from the fiery furnace. You believe He wants to restore your relationships, heal your body, and mend your broken heart. Without wavering—no matter how impossible your situation seems—you believe God will keep His promises. You believe *before* you receive. You believe He will.

Heavenly Father, forgive me for trying to understand the mysteries of your kingdom as a prerequisite for believing in your promises. Thank you for opening my eyes to all your great examples of faith, both Bible heroes and regular people you have put in my path to learn from. Please, Lord, help me not to be moved by my impossible circumstances. Help me not to lose heart and give in to hopelessness and despair. Give me the pure and simple faith of a child, that I might believe it is your will and desire to care for me and rescue me. Help me not to waver. Help me to believe your promises, fully expecting to receive. In Jesus' name, amen.

Night Stalkers Don't Quit

Do not throw away this confident trust in the Lord, no matter what happens. Remember the great reward it brings you!

—Hebrews 10:35

The call came on a Wednesday morning. My dearest friend's worst nightmare was confirmed. Her son Corey was piloting the Chinook helicopter shot down by a Taliban-fired rocket-propelled grenade in eastern Afghanistan the day before. Heavy fighting, high winds, heavy rain, and rugged terrain in the snow-covered Hindu Kush mountains delayed the search and recovery process. For the next seventy-two hours she cried out to God, pleading desperately for the lives of her son and the fifteen others on board. She prayed for peace and strength to sustain her through the unbearable time of waiting for word of survivors.

Even in the absence of official answers, a flood of friends and family members offering condolences, and reporters eager for a story, descended upon her home. In spite of all the reasons for hopelessness, she held on to hope. She prayed for a miracle. And she prayed for assurance that Corey knew the Lord. In answer to her prayer, she learned from his wife that he had committed his life to Jesus. At Corey's suggestion, they were doing Bible study together by email. They prayed together on the phone and exchanged email prayers.

On Friday morning, the call finally came. Every mother's fear became a reality. Her son had perished in the crash. In his honor and memory, the governor ordered all flags in the state to be flown at half-mast on the day of the funeral. The governor attended, along with members of the U.S. Congress and high-ranking military officers, including a four-star general. He received full military honors. The lone sound of taps could be heard at the gravesite while I watched his mother, his wife, and his two sons all receive the carefully folded flag, his numerous medals, and heartfelt words of comfort and thanks from the attending military officials.

Corey was thirty-five years old; he had served his country as an Army aviator for over fourteen years. He spent his last seven years of service flying Special Forces commandos behind enemy lines under cover of night with an elite special operations force called the Night Stalkers. Corey died true to the Night Stalker motto: *Night Stalkers Don't Quit (NSDQ)*. His final mission was to rescue an elite special operations team fighting terrorists still operating in the Kunar province of Afghanistan. In the greatest act of love and obedience, he laid down his life for his friends (John 15:12–13).

Corey loved the Lord and understood authority. He was privy to classified information he could never share, not even with his wife. He is a true hero, a devoted husband, son, father, and friend. As I worshiped the morning after the funeral, his dedication and sacrifice became highly personal. People like him make it possible for me to raise my hands every Sunday at church and freely give praise and worship to my Lord and King. I am humbled that God has placed people in our midst who are willing to place themselves in harm's way to protect and defend our freedom.

Corey would have been proud of his mom. True to his Night Stalker creed, she didn't quit. She didn't stop praying when the situation appeared impossible, when the media and everyone around her called it quits. When her worst fears were realized, *she didn't quit on God*. She didn't turn her back on Him because her prayers weren't answered the way she expected. By faith in His perfect plan, she knows her son is walking on streets of gold. She knows she will be reunited with him someday in that place where there will be no more death, sorrow, crying, or pain, where the old world and its evils are gone forever (Revelations 21:3–4).

She knows this because two thousand years ago there was another mother who believed. When the angel Gabriel told this young virgin girl she would become pregnant and give birth to an eternal King, she simply said, "I am the Lord's servant, and I am willing to accept whatever he wants" (Luke 1:38). When shepherds told her that armies of angels appeared in the heavens singing praises to her newborn son, she quietly treasured these things in her heart (Luke 2:19).

As He grew into manhood, He had an intimate relationship with His Father. He understood authority. When He reached His early thirties, the time came for Him to fulfill His earthly mission. His mother watched Him heal the sick, bring hope to the suffering, and set the captives free. Then, the words of the prophet Simeon came to pass. A sword pierced her very soul (Luke 2:34–35). She watched Him beaten beyond recognition. She grieved His violent, bloody death on a cross. His name was Jesus, and He died for the sins of the world.

Perhaps today, in the mission of life, you feel as though you too have been shot down. The flames engulf you, and you fear you are losing the battle. If you are tempted to abandon your faith, think about these two mothers. Neither one let her own inability to grasp the wisdom and scope of God's plan stand in the way of her faith. Mary's son, the Son of God, was obedient unto death and was rewarded by sitting in the place of highest honor beside God's throne in heaven. Corey died a hero's death for our earthly freedom. Because of the death and resurrection of his beloved Jesus, there is an eternal freedom for Corey and all those who call Him Lord and Savior.

Today, when the enemy is closing in and all hope is lost,

remember Corey's sacrifice. Honor him by keeping your eyes on Jesus, on whom your faith depends from start to finish. Remember the great reward it brings you. The Lord conquered death so you can live with Him forever in that place where there is no more pain and suffering. Think about all He endured so that you don't become weary and give up (Hebrews 12:2–3). When the faith test comes, hold on. No matter what happens, NSDQ.

Heavenly Father, forgive me for giving up on you. Forgive me for doubting your plan and your purposes when my prayers aren't answered the way I expect them to be. Thank you, Lord, for all those who have willingly sacrificed their lives so I can freely worship you. I thank you for your Son, who died to save me from my sin and give me an eternity with you in a place where there is no more death, sorrow, crying, or pain. Please, Lord, give me strength to hold on to my faith, no matter what happens. Help me not to quit when everything around me appears hopeless. Help me to know, when everything is lost, you will never leave me or forsake me. Help me to know you are all I need. In Jesus' name, amen.

Author's note: Chief Warrant Officer Corey J. Goodnature died a hero in eastern Afghanistan on Tuesday, June 28, 2005, while protecting his country and fighting for freedom.

DROP YOUR CRUTCH
THE TRUST TEST

*But blessed are those who trust in the Lord and have made
the Lord their hope and confidence.*

—JEREMIAH 17:7

WHERE DOES YOUR HELP COME FROM?

I look up to the mountains—does my help come from there? My help comes from the LORD, who made the heavens and the earth!

—PSALM 121:1–2

He stared at the phone. The call would come soon. Months of hard work—networking, searching and applying for jobs, following up on leads—it would soon be over. No more worries about house payments, car repairs, health insurance, or college tuition. He had done everything according to the book—phone calls, long lunches, and relationships cultivated with internal contacts. "The job is a cinch," they said. His mind wandered to the things he would do his first few months on the job, how he would build trust with his direct reports and deliver on the promises he made in the interview process.

The phone rang. His heart beat faster as he exchanged pleasantries with his soon-to-be new boss. "I'm sorry, Howie, but we decided . . ." The rest of the conversation trailed off into the darkness as he tumbled deeper and deeper into the pit of despair and disbelief. This cycle would repeat itself seven more times over the course of the next twelve months. Somewhere in the heat of the fire he dropped his crutch. He stopped trusting the job prospects, the sophisticated interviewing techniques, the new pinstripe suit, and the influential networking contacts. He stopped putting his hope in each new job lead. He started trusting the One who created the opportunities, the One who promised to meet all his needs (Philippians 4:19).

Another day—another anxious time of waiting. She rocked back and forth in her chair as she waited for the nurse to call her name. The last six months were a blur, each day blending into the next, each week without a beginning or an end. How many hours had she spent in this place, waiting for doctors, waiting for scans and blood tests, waiting for nurses to administer powerful drugs to kill the cancer cells waging their relentless attack on her body? She had lost count. But today would be the turning point. Today she would know if the new chemo regimen was working.

She tried not to worry. When her hometown doctors offered no hope, she sought out the best cancer center, with the best doctors, in the country. "We have a promising new treatment," they told her. Surely they had the answer. They had the newest drugs and the latest medical knowledge at their disposal. Could today be the turning point, the beginning of her recovery? She dared to let her mind entertain the prospects of her life returning to normal.

"Carol?" She jumped as the nurse repeated her name. She followed the nurse and took her seat in the examination room. More waiting. An eternity passed as the pit in her stomach grew larger. When the doctor finally entered the room, she searched his face for signs of good news. She knew before he spoke. "Carol," he said softly, "the tumor isn't responding like we'd hoped." She felt the floor open up beneath her as she plunged into a dark, bottomless pit. His words about trying a different drug or another treatment sounded distant and muffled, as though she were listening from under deep water. Several more months passed. More waiting. Waiting for doctors, waiting for scans and blood tests, waiting for nurses to infuse the latest drug treatments. Somewhere in the heat of the fire she dropped her crutch. She stopped putting her hope in the drugs, the doctors, and all their medical knowledge.

She started trusting the One who created the medical realm and all its wonder, the One who promised never to leave or forsake her (Hebrews 13:5).

It can be so easy in the heat of battle to let our trust slip from the Creator of all things to the things He created. When we trust anything but God for our supply—our food, protection, or health—idolatry has subtly entered our hearts. Idolatry? How can that be? When we think of idolatry, we often think of Buddha statues and Asherah poles. But God warned us through the prophet Ezekiel to repent and turn away from a different kind of idol—the unseen idols in our hearts (Ezekiel 14:3–8). Paul further cautions us not to turn away from the glorious ever-living God to worship idols and the things that God made (Romans 1:21–25). We become painfully aware of how much trust we place in the idols of our hearts when the blessings of God are suddenly removed and the stool crumbles beneath us.

Howie and Carol both learned how subtly their trust could shift away from God. It can happen to anyone. It happened to Eli, a great judge and priest of Israel. The Philistine army had just attacked and defeated the army of Israel, killing four thousand men, when the leaders of Israel had a brilliant idea: "Let's bring the Ark of the Covenant of the Lord from Shiloh. If we carry it into battle with us, *it* will save us from our enemies" (1 Samuel 4:3, emphasis mine).

So they sent men to Shiloh to get it. They unlawfully entered the Most Holy Place, the sacred part of the temple that only the high priest was allowed to enter once a year. Eli's own sons, Hophni and Phinehas, helped carry it to the battlefield. But in spite of their confidence, Israel lost the battle. Some thirty thousand men were killed, including the sons of Eli. To make matters even worse, the Philistines captured the sacred Ark of God. Eli fell and died when he heard the news (1 Samuel 4:4–18). What happened? For Eli and the Israelites, the Ark itself had become the source of power and protection, rather than the presence of Almighty God.

Several years later, a young shepherd boy named David fought a Philistine giant. He knew exactly where his help came from. For forty days Goliath strutted back and forth, daring some Israelite to come and fight him to determine which army would be subject to the other (1 Samuel 17:1–16). David didn't see a giant, but a mortal man mocking and cursing the God he loved (1 Samuel 17:26). At David's persistence, King Saul agreed to let him fight the giant, and he gave him his own armor for protection. But after trying it on, David stripped off the armor and faced the taunting giant with nothing but a rock, a sling, and a shepherd's staff (1 Samuel 17:32–44).

"You come to me with sword, spear, and javelin, but I come to you in the name of the Lord Almighty—the God of the armies of Israel, whom you have defied. Today the Lord will conquer you. . . . And everyone will know that the Lord does not need weapons to rescue his people. It is his battle, not ours. The Lord will give you to us!" (1 Samuel 17:45–47). Sure enough, with a single shot to the forehead, the Lord gave David his victory.

Whatever battle you're fighting today, it does not belong to you. The Lord does not need your weapons to fight it. You want so desperately to trust the things you can see and hear, feel, and control. You cling to the idols of your heart—your own resources, your own strength, and the support of a doctor, a spouse, or a friend—the weapons of this world. But ever so slowly, it all slips out from under you. Tenderly He speaks to you through the roaring fire. He wants to know: *Am I your supply? Can you trust me alone? Can you drop everything else you trust in my place? Do you dare shift your eyes from the mountain of worldly help to the One who created the heavens and the earth?*

Howie and Carol looked to the mountain, but somewhere in

the midst of their suffering they discovered only God could save them (Psalm 33:20). Do you dare to shed your armor? Only then can you face your giant. Only then, when the world has nothing more to offer, can you know the joy of trusting His unlimited power and provision. Only then will you know . . . your help comes from the Lord.

Heavenly Father, only you can save me! Forgive me for trusting the unseen idols of my heart and for putting my trust in the weapons of this world. My battle is yours to fight. I lay my armor at your feet. I drop my crutch. Thank you, Lord, that you alone are my supply and my protection. I have no earthly need you won't supply from your glorious riches. Lord, please give me a heart like David—a heart that burns for you and always trusts you in times of trouble. In Jesus' name, amen.

Just Ask

Gideon replied, "If you are truly going to help me, show me a sign
to prove that it is really the LORD speaking to me."

—Judges 6:17

He was a farmer named Gideon, forced to thresh wheat at the
bottom of a winepress to hide the grain from the cruel Midianites.
They had driven the Israelites into hiding in the caves and dens of
the mountains, destroying their crops and livestock and reducing
them to starvation. Now, as if things weren't bad enough, the Lord
appeared to Gideon with an impossible assignment: "Go rescue
Israel from the Midianites. I am sending you." Gideon was
stunned. "Me? But I am the last person you should send! My clan
is the weakest and I am the least in my entire family!" The Lord
assured him. "I will be with you. And you will destroy the Midianites as if you were fighting against one man" (Judges 6:16).

Even though God promised to provide all the strength and
tools he needed, Gideon asked for proof that God could be
trusted. Three times, in fact. We might get a little nervous asking
God for proof, but Gideon didn't flinch. First, he wasn't sure if it
was God speaking at all, so he demanded a sign. He asked the
angel of the Lord to wait for him to go home and prepare an
offering of meat and bread. When he returned, the angel had him
place the offering on a rock. The angel touched the offering with
his staff and the entire offering was consumed in flames (Judges
6:17–21).

Gideon was convinced. That is, until the entire armies of
Midian, Amelek, and the people of the east formed an alliance
against his country. They were camped in the valley of Jezreel,
ready for attack, when Gideon demanded another sign. "Lord, if
you are really going to use me to rescue Israel, let this fleece of
wool I lay out on the threshing floor be wet with dew in the
morning, but let the ground be dry." And it was. Then Gideon
did the unthinkable. He asked for another miracle. "Lord, this
night, let the fleece be dry and the ground be wet when morning
comes." I can almost see Gideon covering his head, waiting for the
Lord to send down lighting bolts from heaven. But God, in His
mercy, again answered his request (Judges 6:33–40).

Once more, Gideon was convinced. His army of thirty-two
thousand men would surely defeat the Midianite armies. Then
came the big test. I can only imagine what he thought when the
Lord told him to send home twenty-two thousand of his men
(Judges 7:3). The Lord said, "If I let all of you fight the Midianites, the Israelites will boast to me that they saved themselves by
their own strength" (Judges 7:2). Then, just to make sure Gideon
knew where the victory would come from, the Lord asked him to
send home all but three hundred men (Judges 7:7). Gideon
obeyed. The night of the battle, God gave Gideon one more sign.
He let him slip into the enemy camp and overhear a conversation
that gave him courage. The next day, Gideon's little army of three
hundred Israelites defeated all the vast armies of Midian.

Perhaps you feel a bit like Gideon, woefully unprepared and
inadequate to face your battle today. Gideon's ancestors certainly
did. The Israelites would have entered the Promised Land forty
years earlier if their doubt hadn't pushed them back into the wilderness. They refused to trust God to defeat the giants of the land,
even after He had parted the Red Sea, provided for their daily
needs, and performed extraordinary miracles right before their
eyes (Deuteronomy 1:26–33; Numbers 14:34–35).

But God knew Gideon's heart. Gideon wasn't challenging God to prove He could be trusted. Gideon was crying out to ask God to strengthen his own weak and wavering trust. God didn't condemn his uncertainty or ignore his cries. Step by step, God met Gideon at his point of weakness. He revealed His will and His faithfulness. And slowly Gideon learned to trust Him. In the final hour, he dropped his crutch and leaned on God. God won the victory and the glory.

Okay, so these are Bible times. God doesn't give us supernatural signs anymore when our trust is shaky and we're desperate for assurances. Or does He? In the heat of your fire today, do you long for a sign He has not forgotten you—that you can trust Him to do what He promised? Tom did. He lay in a hospital bed for weeks while doctors desperately tried to find a remedy for the severe inflammation that was eating away his diseased intestines. Each day, he lost more and more weight as his test results and prognosis took a dismal turn.

Finally, as the pain became more and more excruciating, he cried out to God, "Are you going to help me? Can I trust you?" Several times that day and into the evening, he asked the same question. "Can I trust you?" He drifted in and out of sleep that night until finally, close to midnight, His answer came. "Of course you can trust me." Tom heard an audible voice. He immediately repented of his lack of trust and thanked God for all the blessings in his life. That night Tom sat at the feet of Jesus, in the very presence of Almighty God. The next morning brought the doctors a glimmer of hope; the test results looked better. And the next day they looked even more promising. God, in His mercy, met Tom at his place of weakness. He revealed His faithfulness. When Tom's stool crumbled, God showed His power.

He wants your trust too. You want so desperately to give it to Him. You know He can't show you His power while you still cling to the things of this world. If you need God to perfect your lack of trust, just ask Him. Come humbly before Him in prayer. With sincere desire, ask Him to meet you at your point of weakness. Cry out for some supernatural sign that He is still in control, that He has not forgotten you, that you can trust Him with your uncertain future. Then listen and keep watch.

He may not send dramatic signs like those He sent to Gideon or Tom, but they will be dramatic to you. He may send you a friend with a word that only you and God would know its meaning. He may bring you to a certain verse in your Bible and lift it right off the page and into your heart. He may speak to you through a stranger, or supernaturally orchestrate events in your life in ways that only God could do. He may send you a miracle. Go ahead. The next time you wonder if the Lord is really going to help you, just ask.

Heavenly Father, I'm desperate to feel your presence and know you have not abandoned me. Forgive me for my weak and wavering trust. Thank you for meeting me at my point of weakness. Lord, my only hope is in your unfailing love and faithfulness. I need to know you will help me! Give me boldness to ask, and help me trust that you will. Please give me eyes to see you and ears to hear your voice as I cry out in the darkness. Please, Lord, reveal yourself to me. Show me your power! In Jesus' name, amen.

ALL THE STRENGTH YOU NEED

For I can do everything with the help of Christ

who gives me the strength I need.

—PHILIPPIANS 4:13

He was Saul, a brilliant scholar and a Pharisee in good standing. He had received the finest training in Jewish law and tradition. Saul sincerely believed the Christian movement was a danger to Judaism. So he made it his personal mission to hunt down and destroy every follower of Jesus. Like his colleagues at the time, his intellect and social standing blinded him to some three hundred prophesies that spoke of the coming of the Messiah. The Creator of the universe came down to earth, exactly as Saul's beloved Scriptures described He would come—and he missed it. That is, until the Lord stopped him dead in his tracks.

It happened on the road to Damascus. Saul was traveling there with permission from the high priest to arrest Christians and bring them back to Jerusalem in chains. Suddenly, a brilliant light beamed down on him and the Lord himself demanded to know why Saul was persecuting Him. Saul came face-to-face with the transforming power of Jesus Christ (Acts 9:1–19). It was there God began to shift the focus of his fierce passion from persecuting Christians to preaching about Christ. Later, Saul became known as Paul, the apostle to the Gentiles. His worldwide ministry stretched throughout the Roman Empire and into the hearts of every believer through his New Testament letters to the early church.

Life after Paul's conversion couldn't have been easy. Early in his ministry, his Pharisee friends were not too pleased with his defection, and you can imagine the followers of Jesus didn't welcome him with open arms. He spent three years in the desert region of Arabia to be alone with God and to let the dust settle (Galatians 1:17–24).

Later, Paul suffered many fiery trials in his service to Christ. During his missionary journeys, he faced angry mobs, dangerous deserts, and stormy seas. Numerous times he was whipped, beaten, bound in chains, and thrown into prison. He was stoned, shipwrecked, and robbed. He spent many painful and sleepless nights without food, water, or enough clothing to keep him warm (2 Corinthians 11:23–27).

As if the circumstances he faced weren't difficult enough, Paul was afflicted with a thorn in his flesh that was thought to be some sort of debilitating physical ailment. He asked the Lord to remove it three times, and three times the Lord said no. "My gracious favor is all you need. My power works best in your weakness" (2 Corinthians 12:9). This ailment was a hindrance to his ministry, but Paul performed extraordinary miracles in spite of it. His suffering kept him humble and made him depend on God instead of his own skills and abilities.

Just think. This brilliant, self-reliant, highly esteemed Jewish leader could have stayed in the comforts of home, enjoying the company of priests and kings. Instead, he found himself crushed, overwhelmed, and fully expecting to die. He learned he could do nothing to help himself, so he trusted God. The Lord's power alone delivered Paul from mortal danger (2 Corinthians 1:8–10). Paul counted all his impressive human abilities, achievements, and credentials as worthless garbage compared with the greatness of knowing Christ (Philippians 3:4–8). He knew he could do nothing apart from Him (John 15:5).

Before the cancer diagnosis, I was a little like Paul. Maybe I wasn't a brilliant scholar, but I certainly shared his fierce intensity. I attributed my good marriage, well-behaved kids, and a successful career to a lot of hard work and natural ability. With careful planning, I could field client phone calls, do six loads of laundry, clean the house, shop for groceries, go to a couple of school events, and entertain guests for dinner without missing a beat. Success and my own competence blinded me to my need for God's presence in my daily life. That is, until God stopped me dead in my tracks on my own road to Damascus.

It started the day my doctor found a lump in my breast. Even then, I was determined to rescue myself. I read every scientific article and book on breast cancer I could get my hands on, as if my healthcare background and all my research would somehow allow me to prove the doctors wrong. When the diagnosis was confirmed, all my knowledge and ability, everything I knew and trusted, was stripped away. My best-laid plans couldn't save me. I couldn't even trust my own body. All I could do was trust God. In His mercy, He healed my cancer. But He left a thorn deep within my soul. It keeps me on my knees at the feet of Christ. It is a constant reminder that I do nothing on my own strength. In this place of weakness, His power works best.

It's human nature to not need God or notice His presence when we think we are strong and wise. Saul and his Pharisee friends let their superior intellect and social standing keep them from noticing the Messiah when He was right under their noses! It took a road-to-Damascus experience to begin Paul's journey into the very heart of God.

Maybe you haven't had a dramatic personal encounter with God lately but you're feeling the heat. What skills and abilities are you leaning on instead of God? Maybe it's a failing business you're facing. If you can just juggle your creditors, break into that new market, or invest more time, you're certain you can turn things around. Maybe your marriage is falling apart. If you can just make yourself more lovable, more indispensable, or more beautiful, you could win back your spouse's affection.

Or maybe, when the legs on the stool fall out from under you—when you try harder and harder but your best efforts fail you—maybe then you'll notice Him. He's been there all along. Can you hear His voice calling through the fire? *It's okay, you can trust me. Come, rest in my arms. Let me be your strength.* Wherever you are in the furnace of suffering, the power of Christ works best in your weakness. Let Him be the source of your courage and hope. Don't depend on your own understanding or be impressed with your own wisdom (Proverbs 3:5–8). He's all the strength you need.

Heavenly Father, forgive me for depending on my own knowledge, abilities, and credentials to save me instead of trusting you. I know you are the source of all my power and strength, and I do nothing on my own. Everything in this world is worthless compared to the privilege of knowing you and sitting at your feet. I trust you with all my heart and soul. Thank you, Lord, that in my weakness your power works best. Please, keep me on my knees, Lord. Let me see your face in the middle of the fire. In Jesus' name, amen.

FULLY COMMITTED

The eyes of the Lord search the whole earth in order to strengthen

those whose hearts are fully committed to him.

—2 CHRONICLES 16:9

After the united kingdom of Israel was divided under the poor leadership of Solomon's son Rehoboam (1 Kings 12:1–20), both nations followed a path of corruption, idolatry, and evil rulers that eventually led to their collapse. The northern kingdom of Israel fell first (2 Kings 17:1–23), but the southern kingdom of Judah had its share of evil kings. Eventually, their failure to repent brought seventy years of captivity in Babylon (2 Chronicles 36:17–21).

King Asa was one of the good guys. God gave him rest from his enemies because he removed the pagan altars and shrines, cut down the Asherah poles, and obeyed the Lord (2 Chronicles 14:1–7). When an Ethiopian named Zerah attacked his kingdom with an army of a million men and three hundred chariots, Asa sent his courageous troops to meet them. But he knew they were greatly outnumbered and faced impossible odds. Desperately, he cried out to God. "O Lord, no one but you can help the powerless against the mighty! Help us, O Lord our God, for we trust in you alone" (2 Chronicles 14:11).

And the Lord was faithful. He delivered a solid victory over the Ethiopians, and the army of Judah carried off vast quantities of plunder (2 Chronicles 14:12–15). After the battle, the prophet Azariah encouraged Asa to keep up the good work and stay close to God. So Asa removed the idols from the towns he had captured, deposed his idolatrous grandmother from the throne, and repaired the altar of the Lord. Then, with trumpets blaring and horns sounding, Judah under his leadership entered into a covenant to seek the Lord with all their heart and soul (2 Chronicles 15:1–19).

All was well until the final years of Asa's reign. After thirty-five years of peace in the land and steadfast trust in the Lord, he slipped. Some would call it an honest mistake, because it made perfect sense at the time. It started when King Baasha of Israel invaded Judah and prevented anyone from entering or leaving. The peace and economy of Asa's kingdom was threatened. Instead of turning to the Lord, however, he took silver and gold from the treasuries of the Lord's temple and formed an alliance with King Ben-hadad of Aram.

His plan worked brilliantly. King Ben-hadad attacked and defeated King Baasha and drove him out of Judah (2 Chronicles 16:1–6). But God was *not* pleased. He responded to Asa through the prophet Hanani: "The eyes of the Lord search the whole earth in order to strengthen those whose hearts are fully committed to him. What a fool you have been! From now on, you will be at war" (2 Chronicles 16:7–9).

Ouch. That seems like a steep price to pay for failing the trust test. No, it's not a sin to seek help from others when fighting our battles. God created the brilliant doctors and wise counselors. He doesn't expect us to stand by, paralyzed and helpless. When King Sennacherib of Assyria attacked King Hezekiah some two hundred years later, Hezekiah consulted with his officials and advisors and forged a brilliant military strategy. But all along, He committed the entire situation to God in prayer and trusted Him for the outcome (2 Chronicles 32:1–8).

By contrast, in the heat of the fire, Asa put his trust in a powerful king instead of the Lord. He joined all the other kings of Israel and Judah who formed alliances with pagan nations and evil people to protect them. He had completely forgotten the Lord's defeat over the Ethiopians and missed his chance to destroy the army of Aram (2 Chronicles 16:7–8). Asa left God out of his battle. And just as He said would happen, God's peace left the land.

How often do we do the same thing? When Steve came under attack, he thought he understood the importance of cultivating strong relationships. For twenty-five years, he worked closely with his business associates to build a successful sales career. He understood his customers' needs, the motives of his sales force, and how to keep his boss happy. He was shocked when one of his direct reports betrayed him—someone whose job and salary Steve had gone out on a limb to protect. The man had been passed over for Steve's position, so he began to gossip and undermine Steve with the overseas owners.

Steve responded by fortifying his relationship with his own boss, the company president. He thought he had dodged a bullet. All was well . . . until poor market conditions and declining sales sent the company into a tailspin. The owners fired Steve *and* the president. A year and a half of unemployment brought Steve to his knees. During his time in the refining fire, he fortified his relationship with Jesus Christ. He learned to seek and trust Him with all of his heart and soul. And just as there was peace in the land because Asa trusted the Lord, Steve found peace in his heart.

Who do you hope will fight your battle today? Maybe it's a brilliant doctor you hope will save your life, or a powerful boss you hope will save your job or advance your career. Maybe it's a strong spouse, a clever friend, or a "take-charge" parent or sibling who has always come to the rescue in your time of need.

Yes, you can put your confidence in powerful kings, but there is no help for you there. When their breathing stops, they return to dust, and in a moment all their plans come to an end (Psalm

146:3–4). Or maybe you'll form an alliance with God—a relationship that stands the test of time with an Eternal King that never changes (Hebrews 13:8). His eyes search the whole earth. He can see into your fire and into your heart. Will He see a heart that is fully committed?

Heavenly Father, forgive me for putting my trust in powerful people instead of you. Forgive me for leaving you out of my battle plans. People will disappoint me, Lord, but you will never fail me. I invite you into the middle of my fire, and I trust you for the outcome. I long for a deeper relationship with you, Lord. I want to know your mind and your heart. Thank you that you are a God who never changes, and I can always trust in your faithfulness. Please give me a heart that is fully committed to you alone, a heart filled with your perfect peace. In Jesus' name, amen.

GOD ALONE

Let your unfailing love surround us, Lord,

for our hope is in you alone.

—PSALM 33:22

"My God has never let me down." I was shocked to hear those words come out of my mouth. Judging from the expression on her face, so was my "healing coach." She was an expert in holistic approaches for treating cancer patients. I stared at the list of treatments she offered to complement my standard medical treatment for breast cancer. I could benefit from guided imagery, relaxation, yoga, reflexology, Qigong, Reiki, Ayurvedic medicine, and various flower remedies. I was invited to awaken my ancient self through cross-dimensional healing, heal myself through mind and body control, embroider healing talisman symbols, or make a healing drum. I even had the opportunity to meet my "power animals" through Shamanic journeying.

In the heat of the fire, I could have been so tempted to "cover my bases." Sure, I'm a Christian, but what could be the harm in adding some of these "complementary" approaches to the mix? Somewhere deep inside me, I felt a silent alarm going off. I remembered the first commandment. "Do not worship any other gods besides me. Do not make idols of any kind, whether in the shape of birds or animals or fish. You must never worship or bow down to them, for I, the Lord your God, am a jealous God who will not share your affection with any other god!" (Exodus 20:3–5a).

When Moses brought God's commandments down from Mount Sinai, the people had just come from Egypt. They were used to worshiping many gods to get the maximum number of blessings, so it wasn't hard for them to add another god to the list. But when they realized what God really meant—that they were to worship only Him—it was a different story. They spent forty years wandering in the desert because they failed to trust the one true God to meet all their needs.

Daniel's friends—Shadrach, Meshach, and Abednego—faced the same fiery test, only they faced *real* fire. Over twenty-five hundred years ago, Nebuchadnezzar conquered Judah and brought these four men back to Babylon as captives. But God, in His mercy, blessed them with an unusual aptitude for learning literature and science. The king was so impressed that he appointed them to his staff of advisors (Daniel 1:3–21). After amazing the king with his special ability to interpret dreams, Daniel became ruler over all of Babylon and appointed Shadrach, Meshach, and Abednego to be in charge of all the affairs in the province (Daniel 2:1–48).

Life in captivity was going along as well as could be expected until the king erected a ninety-foot-tall gold statue and demanded people of all races and nations to bow down and worship it. Anyone refusing to obey upon hearing the sound of musical instruments would immediately be thrown into a blazing furnace.

Everyone bowed and worshiped the king's statue on cue—except Shadrach, Meshach, and Abednego. When King Nebuchadnezzar heard of their disobedience he was furious. He gave them one last chance to bow to the statue (Daniel 3:1–15). They still refused. "If we are thrown into the blazing furnace, the God whom we serve is able to save us. He will rescue us from your power, Your Majesty. But even if he doesn't, Your Majesty can be sure that we will never serve your gods or worship the gold statue you have set up" (Daniel 3:17–18).

The king was so enraged by their refusal that he heated the furnace seven times hotter, and ordered his strongest soldiers to bind up the three men and throw them into the roaring flames. The intense heat instantly killed the soldiers who threw them in the fire. But to the king's surprise, four men walked around unbound in the furnace, and one looked like a supernatural being. Sure enough, the Lord rescued Shadrach, Meshach, and Abednego from the fiery furnace. They emerged completely untouched by the fire and heat (Daniel 3:25–27).

The king was amazed these men would defy his command and be willing to die rather than serve any god other than the one true God. How many of us would have been tempted to bow down to save our own lives? *Maybe I could bow down just this once, and then ask for forgiveness. What would it hurt? After all, God knows my heart. He knows what I really believe. Besides, this is a crisis! What choice do I have? What if this healing coach is on to something?* Shadrach, Meshach, and Abednego knew their destiny was in God's hands alone. They trusted God to save them, *even if He didn't.* They had experienced His grace and His unfailing love. He is still worthy of our trust, whether or not He intervenes in the way we expect. Shadrach, Meshach, and Abednego stood with God, no matter what the cost.

"My God has never let me down." The moment I blurted out these bold words, I knew, in the depths of my spirit, that I had passed some sort of divine test. I could almost hear the angels clapping and cheering in heaven. Oh, how easy it would have been to turn my back on God and justify my lack of trust. I could have been angry. After all, where was He when the cancer was growing?

But somehow I knew the question wasn't *what* would it hurt for me to trust in a smorgasbord of New Age treatments, but *who* would it hurt? God alone will rescue me in times of trouble and supply my every need (Psalm 33:20; Philippians 4:19). And because of His unfailing and extravagant love for me, I have a unique personal relationship with Him through Jesus Christ. To add anything to the work of the cross—to trust anything else—is the same as believing His blood isn't enough to save me.

In the heat of your suffering, will you pass the trust test? Will you take your stand with God, no matter what the cost? The world will offer you plenty of opportunities to escape the fiery furnace on your own power or through the power of other spirits. You can find books, courses, counselors, chemicals, and empty promises on every corner. Even Jesus was pressured by Satan in the wilderness to trade His suffering for the things of this world.

If our hearts are hardened and we are blind and deaf to the things of God, we are easily led astray (Matthew 13:15). But you have Christ in your heart. You have the power to recognize His voice in all the confusion. You have the same power that rescued Shadrach, Meshach, and Abednego from the fiery furnace and raised Christ from the dead (Ephesians 1:18–20). Those who follow Him will withstand the roaring fire. The world can crumble out from underneath you, and your future is still secure because it rests on a solid foundation that cannot be destroyed (Matthew 7:24–27). Take your stand with Jesus. He won't let you down. Your hope is in God alone.

Heavenly Father, forgive me for sharing my affection with any other god but you and for trusting any spirit other than yours. You are the one true God who meets all my needs. Thank you, Father, for the gift of your Son. His blood is more than enough to save me. Please give me spiritual eyes so I can recognize you and your ways in all the confusion and discern the things that are not of you. Help me to trust you, no matter what the cost. In Jesus' name, amen.

Know He Is God

The "Why Me?" Test

For just as the heavens are higher than the earth, so are my ways higher than your ways and my thoughts higher than your thoughts.

—Isaiah 55:9

His Work is Perfect

He is the Rock; his work is perfect. Everything he does is just and fair. He is a faithful God who does no wrong; how just and upright he is!

—Deuteronomy 32:4

A mother sits quietly, her gaze moving around the room at a large family gathering shortly after the memorial service for her only son. Her eyes rest on her nephews, laughing and joking with each other, hashing over memories of a family vacation taken years past. As their mothers talk, she picks up snippets of conversation—plans for college in the fall, an upcoming wedding, speculation on whether another will be engaged by Christmas. She listens, and she can't help but wonder: *Why, Lord? Why did I have to lose my son and they still have theirs?*

A middle-aged man with a family at home depending on him sits quietly at his weekly Bible study. His eyes scan the room as each person reports on the events of the past week. One shares a particularly difficult situation at work, and several others provide counsel. Another complains about reorganization in his company and why he feels compelled to start looking for a new opportunity. The man can't help but wonder: *Why, Lord? Why did I lose my job after giving it everything I had, and these men are still employed?*

I've been there, and so have you. I'm at a parents' meeting for my daughter's dance team, planning the spring fund-raiser. I'm at the health club working out or in the women's locker room afterward. I'm at a restaurant, a football game, or waiting in line to use the women's rest room. I'm watching all the women around me and I'm wondering: *Why, Lord? Why should my days be filled with doctor visits, cancer treatments, and wigs, while they have their health and hair intact?* Years later, with my health restored, I'm watching while some women suffer cancer recurrences and others pass away. *But Lord, it's not fair!*

Peter had the same thoughts. After Jesus let Peter know the kind of death he would die to glorify God, Peter responded by asking about John, another disciple. "What about him, Lord?" Jesus replied, "If I want him to remain alive until I return, what is that to you? You follow me" (John 21:21–22). Jesus essentially told Peter it was *none of his business* what became of John. Whatever Peter's future might hold, he needed to simply follow Jesus.

Our human tendency is to compare our lives with others, either to rationalize our own level of faithfulness and devotion, or to question God's justice. But God is sovereign. His ways and His thoughts are higher than ours (Isaiah 55:8–9). We get into trouble when we try to elevate our own human understanding of justice and fairness higher than God himself, and then expect Him to meet our standard.

In reality, God *is* the standard. He uses His power according to His own perfection. Whatever He does is fair, regardless of whether we understand it or not. And while we walk on this earth, our human minds may never understand why one person gets cancer and another doesn't, why one person gets healed and another doesn't, or why one person loses a child or a spouse and another doesn't. We may never fully understand why we are suffering while everyone around us seems to be getting a free pass. But we can take comfort in knowing that Jesus is no stranger to our pain. He understands our fears, our disappointments, and our human frailty (Hebrews 2:17–18). And He promised never to leave our side (Matthew 28: 20).

When life isn't fair—when you feel like someone else is getting a better deal than you—keep your eyes fixed on Him. Remember, we are not "cookie cutter" creations. We didn't come into this world off some supernatural assembly line from a one-size-fits-all mold. Every child of God is a perfectly crafted masterpiece, and He has a unique and distinct plan for each one. Jesus had different plans for Peter and John, and both have enriched our lives some two thousand years later.

He has a unique and perfect plan for you too. He knows how dangerous it is for you to take your eyes off Him and start comparing your portion with someone else's. He is more concerned with *your* personal relationship with Him than how He is relating to someone else. As He gently reminded Peter, it's not your concern.

There may be times in your fire when you wonder about your Creator's sense of justice and fairness. You may even think His plan for you is less than perfect. As you read your Bible today, know that it was written just for you. When He tells you that no weapon formed against you will succeed (Isaiah 54:17), when He tells you He heals all your diseases (Psalm 103:3), and when He tells you He will supply all your needs (Philippians 4:19), you can believe Him, because each promise you read—every word of truth—is between you and your God. Resist the temptation to try to figure out what His words mean for others. The Lord said *it's none of your business*. Don't let your failure to understand all His ways rob you of the promises and plans He has for your future. He'll reveal everything you need to know in His appointed time. In the meantime, you can trust He knows what He's doing. Everything He does is just and fair. His work is perfect.

Heavenly Father, forgive me when I compare my own situation to the situations of others. Lord, I know your ways are higher than my ways, and your thoughts are higher than my thoughts. Forgive me when I try to elevate my own limited understanding of justice and fairness to a higher level than yours. Thank you for the gift of your Son, who knows firsthand the depths of my pain and suffering, and who paid the ultimate price so I can have a personal friendship with you. Please help me not to compare this precious relationship I have with you to anyone else's. Help me know that every word I read in the Bible is a personal message, directly from you. Lord, your work is perfect. In Jesus' name, amen.

NO EXEMPTIONS

Here on earth you will have many trials and sorrows. But take

heart, because I have overcome the world.

—JOHN 16:33

Dr. Jack brought joy to everyone who came in contact with him. His family and his entire community dearly loved him. He always went the extra mile for his patients. Unlike many doctors today, he would take time to catch up on the family news, remember their birthdays, call to check on how they were doing, and even schedule appointments after hours when they needed him. Dr. Jack never hesitated to jump in when help was needed. You could find him chairing a community celebration, organizing a fund-raiser for a family in crisis, coaching a youth softball team, or helping a neighbor with a home-improvement project. Dr. Jack was one of the good guys. That's why his cancer diagnosis came as such a shock. Cancer is simply not supposed to happen to people like Dr. Jack. Family and friends from far and wide gathered around to support him. For ten long months of chemo, radiation, and agonizing pain, they hoped and prayed desperately for a miracle. They exhausted every medical option. They fought until they could fight no more. Shortly after Christmas, with his beloved family at his side, Dr. Jack left this world and went home.

In their grief and anger, the family struggled to understand. *Why, God? How could this happen to someone like Dr. Jack? He was such a wonderful husband, father, grandfather, and friend. He had so much life left to live!* I struggled too. I ministered to this family throughout his illness. *Lord, these are good people—people who make a difference, people who care about others. What did they do to deserve this?*

Our limited human minds just can't understand when bad things happen to good people. If we're honest with ourselves, we're much less conflicted when bad things happen to bad people! At some point during my own battle with cancer, I realized that no one was sitting up in heaven keeping track of our good deeds and handing out rewards. We can never "earn" our way into God's favor. It's fortunate that it's not about what we do. How would we ever know when we've done enough or been good enough? Was Dr. Jack good enough? Do we have to be better than him? How much better?

No, it's all about what's been done for us. Jesus died because we can never do enough. We're human, so we can't possibly follow all the rules. No one can (Romans 3:23). The more I learned about God's character and His law, the clearer it became I couldn't obey it (Romans 3:20). I can only be made right with God by believing Jesus sacrificed His life to take away my sins (Romans 3:22–25). In this one ultimate act of unconditional love, God wiped my record clean. It simply doesn't matter how good I am or how many kind things I've done for others. I'm a child of God Almighty, a sinner saved by grace. It's a free gift to all who believe, so none of us can boast (Ephesians 2:8–9).

But what if we're one of the most faithful Christians ever to walk on the face of the earth? Certainly, that kind of person should have a special exemption from pain and suffering! Pastor Lynn is the closest thing to Jesus many people have ever encountered on this side of eternity. Through her prayers and obedient hands, the Lord has healed the sick, fed and clothed the poor, loved the unlovable, comforted the suffering, and restored the brokenhearted. Not just a few people, but hundreds.

After months of prayer, doctoring, and inconclusive tests, word came back that she had cancer. The news rocked the entire church. *Why, Lord? How can someone like Pastor Lynn get cancer? She's not just a good person and a faithful Christian, she's almost a saint!* In our humanness, our shock turned to doubt and fear. *If this can happen to someone as righteous and faithful as Pastor Lynn, then no one is exempt. Oh, Lord, I'm doomed!*

Being a Christian, even a mighty servant like Pastor Lynn, will not guarantee an easy, problem-free life. Jesus himself was spat upon, beaten, misunderstood, betrayed, and crucified. But having a personal relationship with Him *does* guarantee direct access to the throne room of God and a supernatural storehouse of peace in the midst of our trials (John 16:33). We will be pressed on every side by troubles, but He promises we will never be crushed and broken. We may be confused and under attack, but He promises never to abandon us. We fall down, but we get up again and keep on going (2 Corinthians 4:8–9). When we suffer, we share in the death of Jesus. But we also share in His glory when it is displayed for the entire world to see (1 Peter 4:13). If we let Him, God can use our suffering to strengthen and deepen our faith (James 1:2–4). Every trial can be an opportunity for Christ to shine His glory through us (2 Corinthians 4:10).

Jesus shined His glory through Dr. Jack, even though it was not the outcome we prayed for. While he suffered, people were amazed by his peaceful countenance. Many came to know Jesus as a result of his illness. The family began to pray together, read their Bible together, and experience the depth of God's love in brand-new ways.

The Lord used Pastor Lynn's cancer to witness and minister to an entire congregation. She encouraged them not to be angry, but to trust in God's sovereignty. They watched her steadfastly hold on to her faith. Then they watched God work a miracle. Doctors planned to treat a cancer they believed had spread to other organs, but they were surprised to discover only a single self-contained tumor. Pastor Lynn received her healing, but not before God used this long, highly visible journey through uncertainty to strengthen her faith and the faith of all who watched Him carry her through the fire.

Dr. Jack and Pastor Lynn did not deserve cancer, and neither do you. You don't deserve bankruptcy, a failed business, a lost promotion, or a broken marriage either. But think of this: it is only by the grace of God that we receive any blessing in our lives. And it's only by His mercy that we aren't penalized for every sin. Even if your suffering is a consequence of your own choices, you can take comfort in knowing that no amount of personal goodness will ever bridge the gap between your human imperfection and God's perfection. Only by trusting what God has done for you at the cross will you be made whole and perfect in His sight (Ephesians 2:8–10).

When you became a Christian, you secured your eternity in Jesus Christ. As you continue to grow in your faith, His tender mercies start fresh every day (Lamentations 3:22–24). But that still doesn't make you exempt from the world's suffering. Take heart! The fire may burn hot today, but the flames will not consume you. The Lord himself will protect you like a shield (Psalm 33:20). When you step out of the blistering furnace into the light of His presence, you'll discover a deep and everlasting peace—a peace not of this world (John 14:27). You have this confident promise of victory in *every* trial and in *every* sorrow the world throws at you. He has overcome the world.

Heavenly Father, forgive me for blaming you for my suffering and believing that I deserve better. If the fire I am fighting today is the result of my sin, please forgive me! Lord, I know I can never earn my way into your gracious favor. I am not a perfect person and can never become one on my own power. Thank you for your grace and your tender mercies that start fresh every day. Thank you for the gift of your Son, His sacrifice on the cross, and His peace that surpasses all understanding. Thank you for conquering every single trial or sorrow I will ever face in this world. In Jesus' name, amen.

The Potter's Hand

O Israel, can I not do to you as this potter has done to his clay?

As the clay is in the potter's hand, so are you in my hand.

—Jeremiah 18:6

Janice was a cancer survivor. Even as she choked back tears, I could hear the anger in her voice. Five years earlier, she went through treatment for early-stage breast cancer. She was bound and determined she would give this cancer no opportunity to come back into her life. She read every book she could find on cancer. She became obsessive about diet and exercise. She refused to eat or drink anything but organic products purchased at the local health food store. She ran every day. She took great care to avoid anything known or even suspected to be carcinogenic. She had routine exams performed by the best doctors in town, and never left any ache or pain unchecked. She was sure she had conquered her nemesis. And then it came back. Of course Janice was shocked and angry. Who wouldn't be? *How could God let this happen to me again? How could this be possible after everything I did to prevent it?*

We all have a little Janice in us. I know I do. Maybe that's why my own cancer took me so much by surprise. *I have what? That's impossible—I've taken control of my life and I don't have breast cancer on my calendar.* All my efforts to set goals, improve myself, and balance my commitments never once took the possibility of cancer into account. Somewhere in the process of controlling everything else—my schedule, my body, my family, and my career—I thought I could control God. But God will not be controlled. He will not be shaped or molded like clay.

He *is* the potter, and the pot has no right to demand anything from the one who made it. In fact, the pot wouldn't exist if it weren't for the potter! He is the God who made the earth and all the people who live in it. With His hands He stretched out the heavens and commanded the stars in the skies. Do we dare give Him orders about the work of His hands (Isaiah 45:11–12)? I don't think so. Our very breath depends on the life He breathed into us (Genesis 2:7; Job 33:4). If He were to take back His Spirit and withdraw His breath, all humanity would turn to dust (Job 34:14)! He doesn't, because of the extravagant and passionate love He has for His creation; and *nothing*, not all powers of heaven or hell, can ever separate the love of the Father from the children He created (Romans 8:38–39).

Wow. The thought of a God so all-powerful, omnipotent, and merciful almost takes my breath away. As I try to understand His sovereignty, I feel like a child again. Growing up, I simply didn't understand my parents' reasoning. I didn't like their silly rules. Like most teenagers, my aspirations and theirs were often on a collision course. Eventually, I learned they had wisdom far beyond my years, and the boundaries they set for me didn't need explaining. Because I trusted them to take care of me and I knew how much they loved me, I knew their decisions were always in my best interest. It became even clearer after I had teenagers of my own.

The same holds true in our relationship with our heavenly Father. Perhaps you had goals and aspirations—a marriage that would last a lifetime, health that would carry you into your golden years, or a business that would set you up for an early retirement. When our plans are frustrated, and our hopes and dreams go up in smoke, we come face-to-face with God's sovereignty. Like rebellious teens, we demand detailed explanations. But He gives us no answers.

Janice knew that God is not the author of disease and destruction. As she came to understand the sovereign nature of God, she started to see His hand in every detail of her cancer journey. She knew that nothing comes to her that hasn't first passed through His love. She found comfort in knowing that God is wise and good, and His Son is a light of hope in a fallen world. She trusted His promise that something good would come out of her cancer (Romans 8:28) and put her life in the Potter's hands. Just as a young child doesn't question his parents' wisdom, the clay doesn't question the Potter's work (Romans 9: 20–22). She trusted Him to mold and shape her into the kind of pot He wanted her to be.

Are you prepared to let God be God? Will you be clay in the Potter's hand? A potter has total control over the clay. He will continue to work with it until it becomes a useful vessel. As the potter molds and shapes the pot on the wheel, flaws and imperfections often appear on the potter's creation. The potter can allow the defects to stay, or squash the pot into a lump of clay and start over (Jeremiah 18:4).

Perhaps you have your own idea of what the finished pot should look like. Perhaps you've even tried to scrape up the discarded clay off the floor and put it back in an attempt to refashion the Potter's work! He knows everything about you (Psalm 139). You can hide no flaw or no defect from Him. Be receptive to what the Potter wants to teach you. Submit to Him as soft, pliable, moldable clay in the palm of His hand. He'll start reshaping you into the beautiful vessel He envisioned all along, a vessel more stunning than any you could have designed on your own. In His hands you will be delicately detailed and uniquely fashioned to reflect His love and His purpose for creating you—a vessel suitable for the palace of a King.

Heavenly Father, forgive me for assuming I know better than you what is best for me. Forgive me when I try to take charge of my own life without any regard for you and your plans for me. Lord, I am amazed by your love for me. Forgive me when I forget how precious I am in your sight. Thank you for your grace and mercy, and for never leaving my side. Lord, I know you are sovereign over the fire that threatens to consume me, and that nothing comes to me that hasn't passed through your love. Please help me to see you and feel your presence in every detail of my suffering. I yield to you, Lord. You are the Potter. I am soft, pliable clay in the palm of your holy hands. Mold me and shape me into the beautiful vessel you created me to be. In Jesus' name, amen.

FOR HIS GLORY

For everything comes from him;

everything exists by his power and is intended for his glory.

—ROMANS 11:36

For His *glory? But I thought it was all about* me*!* It was, until the firestorm roared into my life and changed everything. In the years before my forty-seventh birthday, I thought I had all I ever wanted. Good marriage, well-behaved kids, a successful career, and a beautiful house; what else did I need? With a little help from my naturally high-achieving, type A perfectionist personality, I had mastered control of it all. Then I learned I had invasive breast cancer. *Why, God? Cancer isn't supposed to happen to me. Cancer happens to other people!*

During the next several months I discovered what I was missing: Jesus. I thought I knew Him before. I went to church on Sunday and, unless there was a crisis, I kept Him conveniently tucked away in the spiritual compartment of my life until the next Sunday. I thought I understood everything He had to show me. All through those years I thought I was a Christian, and I never knew Him at all.

On the day I landed in the fiery furnace, He tenderly reached out His hand through the flames and gave me two choices: I could face my uncertain future on my own or I could trust Him. From the moment I invited Him into the middle of the fire, it became all about Him. He carried me through weeks and months of doctor visits, tests, needles, chemotherapy, radiation, and wigs. In this bald and dark place, I came face-to-face with His holiness and my own brokenness. I learned how desperately I needed a Savior. He was no longer Lord of my Sunday mornings or my current crisis; He became Lord of *my life.*

Jesus Christ won my heart. He healed me. He changed my life for all to see. I teach, write, and speak of Him today for only one reason. He used my time in the fire for *His* glory and *His* purposes. He used what Satan intended for evil and turned it into something good. And this should come as no surprise. Jesus Christ is in the life-changing business. He never stops pursuing us, and He'll do whatever it takes to win our devotion.

He did not change my life for my own benefit. It was not so I could climb the next successful step on the career ladder or because He *needs* me to be an author or to minister to others. God will move in His kingdom and accomplish His purposes, regardless of whether or not I choose to participate. No, it's all for Him. All for *His* glory.

The disciples stood by and watched Jesus radically change one life after another. They too had questions about pain and suffering. One day they noticed a beggar who had been blind since birth. Suffering was considered a result of sin in Jewish culture. So naturally, they wondered if the man's blindness was the result of his own sin or the sin of his parents.

In answer to their question, Jesus said something surprising: "It was not because of his sins or his parents' sins. He was born blind so the power of God could be seen in him" (John 9:2–3). Then He spit on the ground and made mud with the saliva. He smoothed the mud over the blind man's eyes and told him to go wash in the pool of Siloam. When the man went to the pool and washed, sure enough, his sight was restored. Those who watched were amazed. Of course, they were anxious to know more about how it had happened, and who the man was that had brought about such a radical change in the beggar's life (John 9:6–12).

The religious leaders refused to believe the man was healed. They demanded an explanation. They insisted that Jesus could not be of God because He broke the law and healed on the Sabbath (John 9:16). They tried to discredit the man's claim of blindness by demanding the "real" truth from his parents (John 9:18–23). They even accused Jesus of being a sinner (John 9:24). The man insisted that only a man from God could heal the eyes of a blind man. He didn't know any answers to the questions they asked. He didn't *need* to know. He only knew one thing: "I was blind, and now I can see!" (John 9:25). Jesus said this man was blind *so the power of God could be seen* in him. And indeed it was. Jesus changed his life for the entire world to see. Even though his faith was severely tested, the man believed and worshiped Jesus (John 9:38).

It's true; we live in a world where innocent people sometimes suffer. But we also live with an awesome promise. God causes *everything* to work together for the good of those who love Him and are called according to His purposes (Romans 8:28). Will the power of God be seen in you? Imagine yourself in the furnace today. As the flames burn hot, people are watching. Just like the disciples, they may be secretly wondering why the world has been so unfair to you. Today, when God reaches out His hand through the flames, you grab it and hold on tightly. People watch as you walk to your pool of Siloam to cool off from the heat of the fire. They watch as you emerge from the pool with your brokenness restored. They watch as you tell the world how God has changed your life. They watch as you participate with God Almighty in the work of His kingdom. They watch, just as those who witnessed the miracle of the blind beggar. *They want what you have.* They want to learn more about this man who changed your life forever.

Will the power of God be seen in you? Regardless of the reason for your pain, God can use it to demonstrate His power and bring glory to His Son. He can use it to bring you into His presence and closer to His heart. He can use your testimony to touch the life of one or the lives of millions. He can use it for reasons you may never know. But He *will* use it. All for His purposes; all for His glory.

Heavenly Father, forgive me when I think it's all about me. Forgive me when I'm satisfied with your blessings, but I miss you in midst of them. Thank you for your promise that everything works together for the good of those who love you and want to do your will. Lord, I take your hand. Please let your power be seen through my suffering. I know everything comes from you and exists for your purposes. Please, Lord, restore me and change me. Use my life for your glory! In Jesus' name, amen.

WHERE WERE YOU?

Where were you when I laid the foundations of the earth?
Tell me, if you know so much.

—JOB 38:4

It was September 12, 2001. I was devastated, like everyone else.
People all over the world were glued to television sets and Internet
news sites, trying to make sense out of the tragic events that
unfolded before their eyes the day before. Phone lines buzzed and
emails bounced back and forth as we shared our shock and grief
over the senseless loss of innocent life at the hands of hate-filled
terrorists. As I opened and read an email from a nonbelieving
friend, I could almost hear the sarcasm in the words she wrote . . .
"Where was your God yesterday?"

Three years later, this same friend questioned my faith when
thousands of innocent people died in the tsunami in Southeast
Asia. "Where was your God?" How often have you heard people
ask the same thing? Where was God when an innocent child came
into the world with a crippling disease? Where was God when
three teenage sons perished in an auto accident or a disturbed
young student opened gunfire on his classmates in a school cafete-
ria? Where was God when a young mother died of cancer and left
three young children without a mother and a young husband
without a wife? Where was God when the bottom fell out of your
life and you tumbled into the fire? Where is He now, as you battle

the flames that threaten to destroy everything you have left?

Job wanted to know. He was a righteous man who loved God. He lived a life of wealth and prestige until suddenly his livestock, servants, farmhands, home, and all his children were destroyed (Job 1:13–19). After everything was stripped away, he was struck with a dreadful case of boils from head to foot (Job 2:7). As he sat in ashes, scraping his skin with broken pottery, his wife told him to curse God and die (Job 2:8–9). Job questioned what kind of faith he would have if he gave up on God for allowing bad experiences along with the good (Job 2:10).

In his deep anguish, Job did not curse God. Instead, he cursed the day of his birth. He believed it was better to never be born than to be forsaken by Him (Job 3). *Where was God?* Why had He allowed Job's world to crumble despite his right living? His friends came to comfort him, but instead, they offered less than helpful advice. One insisted that sin had caused his suffering and urged him to repent (Job 4–5, 15, 22). Another accused him of not admitting his sin (Job 8, 18, 25). A third friend thought Job deserved to suffer even more (Job 11, 20). But Job maintained his innocence (Job 3:1–31:40). And after testing him as gold in the refiner's fire, he was confident that God would also find him innocent (Job 23:10).

Finally, the Lord spoke to him from a mighty whirlwind. He didn't give Job any answers. Instead, He asked a series of questions Job couldn't possibly answer. *Where were you when I laid the foundations of the earth (Job 38:4)? Have you ever commanded the morning to appear and caused the dawn to rise in the east (Job 38:12)? Who sends the rain that satisfies the parched ground and makes the tender grass spring up (Job 38:27)?* Job realized his limited human mind couldn't even grasp the wonder of God's physical creation. How could he possibly understand God's mind and character? He responded by humbling himself before God (Job 42:1–6). After Job prayed for his friends, God restored him to happiness and health, giving him twice as much as he had before (Job 42:10–16).

Where is God when evil people prosper and innocent people suffer? My friend demanded an answer. While we walk this earth, there may never be an answer. God can rescue us from the fiery furnace or let suffering come for reasons we may never understand. Sometimes it prepares us for a higher calling. Sometimes it's an attack by Satan. Sometimes, like Job, we simply don't know why we suffer.

We will never understand His decisions and His methods. We will never know what the Lord is thinking or be wise enough to give Him advice (Romans 11:33–34). Job let his need to know *why* consume him, until God made it perfectly clear. It's better to know God than to know why. He didn't owe Job an explanation (Job 38–41). Job learned that when everything else is stripped away, God is all he ever had.

Lori learned too. She learned that without God, she couldn't bear to live. Four years after 9/11, the same terrorist group who slammed airplanes into the Twin Towers fired a rocket-propelled grenade at her husband's Chinook helicopter, killing all sixteen crew members on board. They were on a mission to rescue fellow special operations forces engaged in a fierce battle in eastern Afghanistan. When Lori's life went up in flames, she came to a place of complete trust—a place where no more questions stood between her and her God (John 16:23). She no longer needed an explanation for the sacred things still hidden from her. She trusted He would reveal the reason for her grief in His perfect time. When all was lost, she trusted His promise to give her a future and a hope (Jeremiah 29:11). She clung to God because God was all she had left. She knew that everything in this world that gives comfort and joy comes directly from Him. Nothing comes to her without first passing through His love. And if all we have belongs to Him and comes from Him, He's all she ever had.

Where was your God when the bottom fell out of your life and you tumbled into the fire? You can demand an explanation.

You can curse God and give up. Or you can trust God and draw near. Can you hear His voice calling you through the roaring flames? *Where were you? Were you there as the morning stars sang together and all the angels shouted for joy* (Job 38:7)? Where was your God? He tumbled into the fire with you. He's battling the flames right alongside you.

He promised to never leave you or forsake you (Hebrews 13:5). Choose to trust Him. Choose to submit to His sovereignty and rest in His loving arms, even though you don't understand all His ways. The sacred friendship you have with your Lord and Savior is more priceless than all your worldly understanding. He is God. He's all you ever had, and He's all you'll ever need.

Heavenly Father, forgive me when I doubt your wisdom and your sovereignty. Forgive me when I question the reason for my suffering and let my lack of understanding cause me to turn away from you. I know I can't possibly understand your ways. I know the only thing that really matters is my sacred friendship with my Lord and Savior. Thank you for all the blessings that come directly from your loving and generous hands into my life. Lord, everything comes from you. Everything belongs to you. You are all I ever had. You are all I need. Lord, let me rest in your presence. In Jesus' name, amen.

PICK UP YOUR CROSS
THE SURRENDER TEST

Then he said to the crowd,

"If any of you wants to be my follower, you must put aside your

selfish ambition, shoulder your cross daily, and follow me."

—LUKE 9:23

No Middle Ground

Then Jesus turned to the Twelve and asked,

"Are you going to leave, too?"

—JOHN 6:67

Jeff went to church every Sunday. He was raised in the church, and he knew it was the right thing to do. Besides, the kids needed religion. *The world is getting to be a dangerous place,* and he hoped the things they learned in confirmation class and youth group would keep them on the right path. He was an usher and volunteered with his wife in the youth area since they had kids in the program. He felt especially good when he went over and above the call of duty to serve on a special committee or help the less fortunate alongside other church leaders and volunteers. It was a bonus that the large suburban church was a gold mine of business contacts for his booming consulting practice.

He still wasn't sure about the arm raising and clapping that went on during the service. He was certain his parents wouldn't have approved. He watched the people carry their Bibles to church every Sunday, and he noticed all the pages were underlined and marked up with notes. Every week the pastor encouraged the congregation to read their Bibles daily and join a small group of other Christians who would hold them accountable for their faith journey.

Jeff didn't have much time for Bible reading, and he was sure he didn't need a small group. He had lots of friends. Besides, they would expect him to talk about his relationship with Jesus and other "religious matters" that were best kept in private. They might even expect him to pray in public. All this spontaneous praying out loud at meetings and other gatherings made him a little uncomfortable. After all, prayer was a personal thing. As far as Jeff was concerned, the talk he was hearing about Bible studies in the workplace and praying before business meetings was way out of line. *Corporate prayer belongs in the front of the church or possibly in the prayer chapel, where all the people with serious problems go for help.* And this was a place Jeff had no intention of ever going.

In some ways we can all relate to Jeff. He wants to follow Jesus, but he wants to stay exactly where he is—comfortable, secure, unchallenged, and undisturbed. He wants to live life on his own terms. The things of God belong in church and are just another activity on the family's busy schedule. It's much easier to give our time and effort to the goals of this world—results we can control and see—than to devote our lives to Christ.

Besides, some of the teachings of Jesus are really difficult to accept. Many of His own disciples deserted Him because they could not understand how Jesus could be living bread from heaven. They didn't understand the meaning of His words—that if we accept Him into our lives, we are united with Him completely and will live forever (John 6:47–58). It was hard to receive the news that their human effort accomplishes absolutely nothing without the Holy Spirit who gives eternal life (John 6:63).

We too want to ignore His words that challenge us and accept the words that allow us to stay comfortable. But Jesus does not allow us to straddle the fence. He asked the disciples if they planned to leave, only to show there is no middle ground with Him. They had two choices: accept Him as Lord and seek to understand His teaching, or reject Him because they didn't like what they had heard. Many deserted Him. But those who remained realized that Jesus *is* the only way. Peter asked for all of us: "Lord, to whom would we go? You alone have the words that give eternal life" (John 6:68).

We can turn our backs on Him and look elsewhere for eternal life. The world certainly has plenty to offer—money, power, and everything from intellectualism and secular humanism to New Age religions and self-empowerment books. We can stay for all the *wrong* reasons—social status, to feel good about ourselves, to win the approval of family and friends, or for personal gain—and never choose to really follow Him. Or we can stay with Jesus, learn from Him, and let Him transform our lives. To dabble in our faith is like being *almost* pregnant. There can be no such thing . . . we make a commitment to follow Christ or we don't.

Choosing Him is not a matter of my degree of commitment or my level of spiritual maturity. I don't call myself a Christian with the hope that someday I will become a "born-again Christian" or the intention that I will never become one. *All* who accept Him as Lord and Savior are born-again children of God (John 1:12–13). Have you made Jesus the Lord of your life?

A failing business finally brought Jeff to a decision point. For months he struggled. He turned inward, hiding his problem from his family and friends. Admitting failure and downsizing his life-style was simply not an option. As the bills mounted and the mortgage payments slipped further and further past due, he worked every angle within his grasp to generate the cash he needed to save his business, his home, his marriage, and his dignity.

Every angle but Jesus, that is. And Jesus was very clear on the matter. If Jeff wanted to be His follower, he had to put aside his selfish ambition, shoulder his cross, and make a commitment to follow Him (Matthew 16:24). He had to give up his life for Jesus, because following Him requires complete, moment-by-moment submission and doing His will even when the work is difficult. He had to choose Jesus over a life of deceit and self-satisfaction. He had to forfeit his self-centered need to be in control of his life and let the Lord direct his steps. He had to trust that His Creator knows what's best for him. And he had to believe that in giving up his life for Jesus, he would find true and lasting life (Matthew 16:25).

After years of playing church and going through the motions of being a Christ-follower, Jeff decided to become one. He went to the prayer chapel, received Christ as his Lord and Savior, and picked up his cross. The disciples understood the symbolism of shouldering their cross. In Roman culture, condemned criminals had to carry their crosses through the streets to the crucifixion site. Following Jesus meant a true commitment with no turning back. Things were rough at times. We all struggle in our faith journey to keep our commitment to Jesus. But even as he struggled, Jeff didn't look back. With God as the new foundation, and the love and prayers of his faith community, Jeff's marriage and finances were eventually restored. The Lord blessed him with a new job opportunity, where he even started a workplace Bible study. He wanted to share the reason for his hope and his changed life.

Are you going to leave too? Jesus is calling you through the fire. He wants to know. Will you pick up your cross and follow Him? Maybe you're afraid of what He might do, or worse, what He might require of you. You can be like some of His disciples and desert Him. His teaching can be difficult sometimes. You can turn your back on Him and look elsewhere for the answers to your problems. Or like Jeff, you can dabble in your faith and keep Him at a safe distance. But if you continue to protect yourself from the discomfort God might call you to endure, you will never fully experience His power and the life He has planned for you. You will never truly experience what it means to be a follower of Christ.

There is no fence-straddling with Him. You must decide

whether He's Lord of your life or He's not. You will either surrender your right to yourself or you won't. He requires your full
commitment—no turning back. So don't leave. And don't despair
when the road gets rough and you stumble and fall. Stay with Him
and let Him teach you. His ways are gentle and His love never
ends (Matthew 11:28–29; John 1:14). Pick up your cross and follow Him. There is no middle ground.

*Heavenly Father, forgive me when I want to stay comfortable and
secure in my walk with you. Forgive me for wanting to live on my own
terms instead of yours, and for devoting my life to the goals of this
world, instead of devoting my life to you and your purposes for me.
Thank you, Lord, that even in my fire today you have wonderful
plans for my life. Lord, I don't want to straddle the fence anymore. I
want to surrender my life and my will to you. Lord, I pick up my
cross. I accept you, Jesus, as Lord of my life. Please help me to understand your ways. Help me when I'm tempted to turn back. In Jesus'
name, amen.*

THE PLACE OF SURRENDER

The sun rose as he left Peniel,

and he was limping because of his hip.

—GENESIS 32:31

Jacob had a history of control and manipulation. He learned it from his mother, Rebekah. When she was pregnant with twin sons, the Lord told her that the descendents of the older son would serve the descendents of the younger (Genesis 25:23). As the boys grew up, she favored the younger son, Jacob. She was determined to help God's prophetic words come true. She had a little help from the impulsive Esau, who sold his birthright, a special honor given to the firstborn son, to Jacob for a bowl of lentil stew (Genesis 25:28–34).

Later on, Rebekah masterminded a plot to help Jacob steal the family blessing from his older brother. She helped him cleverly disguise himself as Esau. Old and nearly blind, their father Isaac fell for the trick. Instead of blessing his rightful heir, Esau, he gave Jacob an irrevocable blessing, granting him all the land God promised to Abraham's descendents (Genesis 27:1–39).

Esau was so angry that he threatened to kill Jacob as soon as Isaac died (Genesis 27:41). And now, twenty years later, it was time for Jacob to face his brother. Esau was about to meet him in the middle of the desert with an army of four hundred men (Genesis 32:6). Jacob was terrified. He knew God was his only hope, so he cried out to Him for mercy. He thanked Him for blessing his life and reminded Him of His promise to treat him kindly and multiply his descendents until they became too numerous to count. He begged God to come and rescue him from his brother (Genesis 32:7–12).

Jacob sent his wives, children, and all his possessions away from the camp for their protection. While all alone he met an angel of the Lord, who wrestled with him all night long. Jacob wanted God's blessing so badly that he wouldn't let go of the angel. Finally, the angel dislocated Jacob's hip; it was the only way God could overcome his strong will. Jacob had reached a place of complete brokenness and surrender. He would no longer walk in his own strength. He would now walk with a limp, symbolizing his dependence on God alone.

God could now bless Jacob abundantly with the inheritance He had promised long before he and his mother took matters in their own hands (Genesis 28:15). God restored his relationship with Esau and made Jacob the father of the twelve tribes of Israel. Jacob named the place where he wrestled with the angel *Peniel*, meaning "face of God." It was in this place of surrender that he met God face-to-face (Genesis 32:30).

Sometimes God has to take us to Peniel. He might even have to dislocate our hip. Our need to control and manipulate can be so strong that it takes a firestorm of adversity to get our full attention. God did not reject Jacob for his determination and resourcefulness. Beneath his cold and conniving exterior, God saw a humble and repentant heart—a heart God needed to soften in order to prepare Jacob for His call on his life. At Peniel God had His way in Jacob's life. Jacob came to a place of complete consecration to God's will and purposes. And God blessed him greatly.

Where is your Peniel? Mine was cancer. I was a master at running my own life and doing things my own way. Like Jacob, I achieved a lot of earthly success through my own resourcefulness.

But God looked into my heart and saw a future He had planned for me that would never be realized until I fully surrendered to Him and let Him take the lead. Cancer brought me to a place of brokenness. As I wrestled with God, He had to "dislocate my hip" to bring me to a place where I am fully dependent on Him alone. And ever since that day I limped out of Peniel, it keeps me in His presence—seeking His face and His will.

What failure, disappointment, or adversity sent you into the fiery furnace? Perhaps you've lost something dear to your heart, and you can't imagine life without it. Perhaps an overwhelming problem looms over you and you've run out of answers. Maybe someone or something threatens to destroy you and everything you worked for all your life. As the fire roars, you gasp for each breath as the smoke and heat sears your throat and burns your lungs. You grab whatever you can find to beat back the flames. As Jacob did, you cry out desperately to God. You remind Him of His power and His promises and beg Him to come to your rescue. God meets you in the fire and you grab hold of Him. You cling to Him and you don't let go.

What will He have to do to gain your complete surrender? If you continue to wrestle with Him in the fire as Jacob did, if you resist Him because He isn't working in a way that meets your expectations, you may force Him to put you out of joint. He may be using this time to change your old nature and bring you into total dependence on Him. Why? Because only God knows what is best for you. When He looks at you, He sees the beautiful child He created and all the blessings He planned for your life (Romans 12:2).

You will never fully become that person if you continue to live on your own terms. When you trust Him with all your heart and seek His will in all you do, your life can become exactly the way He intended it to be (Proverbs 3:5–6). He can take you from the place of surrender to the place of blessing He planned from the beginning. Let Him transform your heart and your mind. Let Him show you His will and His perfect plans. When the sun rises in Peniel, you may walk out with a limp, but you'll limp into the glorious life you were born to live.

Heavenly Father, forgive me when I control and manipulate my circumstances to make things go my own way. Forgive me when I take matters into my own hands and stand in the way of your perfect plans for me. Lord, thank you for your promises and for blessing my life so abundantly. Thank you for coming to meet me in my fire. I cling to you, Lord. Please change my heart and my mind! Help me to surrender my life to your will and purposes. I want to know the person you created me to be. I want to see your face. In Jesus' name, amen.

NOTHING LEFT STANDING

Jesus felt genuine love for this man as he looked at him.
"You lack only one thing," he told him. "Go and sell
all you have and give the money to the poor, and you
will have treasure in heaven. Then come, follow me."

—MARK 10:21

Each day you cry out for the Lord to come and rescue you from the fire. You want Him to completely extinguish the flames. You want your old life back. You want Him to heal your pain and restore your broken heart. As the days turn into weeks and you walk through the fire in silence, you cling to His promise that it will not burn you; the flames will not consume you (Isaiah 43:2). Imagine today that He does more than put out the flames. Today, He makes an appearance: Jesus Christ, live in the flesh, in the middle of your fire. He looks at you with eyes full of love and compassion and says, "Come. Follow me." Excuse me? He says again, "Come. Follow me."

I don't know how you would react. I'm embarrassed to admit where my thoughts might go. *You mean . . . NOW? Where are we going? You want me to leave my home? But I'm so comfortable here! What about my family? They need me! And what about my work? I have a really important meeting tomorrow. Besides, we're supposed to leave on vacation next week! Follow you? I want to follow you, Lord, but . . .*

You know I'm a really good person. Are you sure there's no other way?

I suppose this is how the rich young man felt, the one who asked Jesus what he had to do to get eternal life. He was a good man who obeyed the commandments. He didn't murder, commit adultery, cheat, or steal. He honored his parents and never testified falsely against his neighbors (Mark 10:17–20). In genuine love, Jesus uncovered the one barrier that could keep this man from following Him: his love for money. "You lack only one thing," He told him. "Go and sell all you have and give the money to the poor, and you will have treasure in heaven. Then come, follow me" (Mark 10:21). Jesus exposed the young man's one weakness: wealth. Wealth represented the young man's pride of accomplishment and all he had earned by his own self-effort. Jesus knew his heart. He knew this man's money mattered more to him than God.

Howie wasn't rich. He was unemployed. He didn't need to be rich. He just needed meaningful work with a reputable company, enough income to support his family and do the things he wanted to do, and enough stored away to retire comfortably. Both his bank account and his retirement investments shrank dramatically post–9/11, as each week and each promising opportunity slipped out of his hands.

Somewhere in the middle of his fourteen-month hiatus in the fire, God prompted him to tithe 10 percent of his unemployment check. *Surely there must be some mistake. Ten percent of what?* The check without the tithe taken off barely covered the house payment, let alone the rest of his living expenses. Howie wrestled with God, and God eventually won. In obedience, Howie gave a tithe of 10 percent. Then, after months of futile job searching and desperation, God finally answered his prayers, but not in the way Howie expected. An offer came from a small, unknown company. It was a lower-level position with considerably less compensation than he was accustomed to earning. In love, Jesus said, "Come.

Follow me." It made no logical sense at the time, but Howie followed.

Jesus exposed his weakness. Howie was proud of his ability to work hard to support his family. He was proud of his sales success, but even more so, of his ability to build relationships and solve his customers' problems. It made him feel good about himself. People needed and respected him. He enjoyed the prestige of the large companies that employed him and the promotions he had earned over the years. Through the fire, he learned that the thrill of success and the rewards that measured it had become more important to him than God.

Gradually, in the years after the fire, God restored his income, his position, and his retirement account. But He did it *His* way, with Christ as the foundation. Howie's commitment to daily Bible reading, prayer time, and a small group of godly men helps ensure that Jesus stays in the center of his life. And he has discovered an amazing thing about God's economy: There always seems to be time in his schedule now to bless and minister to others in need.

Howie learned we have a choice from the moment God makes himself known to us. The ball is in our court. What we do next reflects what we really believe. The rich young ruler chose not to follow Jesus. Ironically, as a successful man of his time, a perfectionist and follower of the law, he wanted to be just *like* Jesus. It grieved him that he could not surrender the one thing that kept him from experiencing the fullness of Christ (Mark 10:22). But Jesus would not share the young ruler's allegiance with any other person or thing. He pointed out the one area of the man's life he had not yet yielded to Him. And He did so in love. *If you are really serious about following me, go and sell all you have.*

If Jesus asked, could you give up your car, house, career, or income? Does God really expect you to go out and sell all your possessions? No, but you cannot allow money or possessions to keep you from following Him. You cannot surrender completely to Jesus while holding on to anything you value more than Him. With love and compassion in His eyes, He may come into your fire and point out the one thing you lack—certain qualities, possessions, or desires in your heart that He wants you to yield to Him. Listen. Can you hear His voice calling in the fire? *Come. Follow me.* Will you surrender to Jesus your rights to anything you hold closer to your heart than Him? Will you come humbly before Him, stripped of everything, completely aware of your need for Him? Will you sell all that you have? If your answer is "yes," then go and follow Him, because there is nothing left standing between you and your God.

Heavenly Father, forgive me when I value my family, my possessions, my accomplishments, or anything else in my life more than my relationship with you. Thank you for your unfailing love and your tender mercies. Thank you for revealing yourself to me. Lord, I come humbly before you. Please look into my heart and show me the one thing I lack—anything that might be standing between us. I want to yield to you, Lord. I want to sell all I have. I want to follow you. In Jesus' name, amen.

A HOLY SACRIFICE

And so, dear brothers and sisters, I plead with you to

give your bodies to God. Let them be a living

and holy sacrifice—the kind he will accept.

—ROMANS 12:1

When God led Moses and the people of Israel out of captivity, He provided for both their physical and spiritual needs. The Tabernacle was their portable place of worship. When it was all completed according to His detailed specifications, a cloud covered it, and the glorious presence of the Lord filled it (Exodus 40:34). When the cloud lifted, the people would set out on their journey, following it. When the cloud stayed over the Temple, they stayed in that spot until it moved again (Exodus 40:36–37). The Tabernacle was God's dwelling place on earth. When King Solomon, David's son, built the magnificent permanent temple in Jerusalem some five hundred years later, it was also filled with the glory and presence of God (2 Chronicles 5:13–14). However, when the Israelites turned their backs on God and traveled down a path of sin and rebellion, His glory left the temple, and enemies destroyed it (2 Kings 25).

After Jesus died on the cross and rose from the dead, God no longer needed a physical dwelling place on earth. We—you and me, the body of believers called the church—became His temple. When we became Christians, the Holy Spirit came to dwell within us. We no longer own the rights to our own bodies (1 Corinthians 6:19) because Jesus bought us for a high price. His death set us free from sin, yes, but it also obligated us to surrender ourselves to God's absolute control.

It is critical that we live in His will if we want to remain in fellowship with God. His death set us free from sin, but it also obligated us to surrender ourselves to God's absolute control. As long as we live in His will, He can remain in fellowship with us. But as the Israelites learned when God's glory left the temple, a holy God cannot stay in relationship with us when we turn our backs on Him and go our separate ways. God is light and there is no darkness in Him (1 John 1:5). As darkness cannot live in the presence of light, sin cannot exist in the presence of a holy God.

Think of it. When you received Christ as your Lord and Savior, the same power that raised Him from the dead took up residence within you (Romans 8:11). If you choose to come under His complete and total authority, the Holy Spirit gives you access to all the powers of heaven and earth. God can't entrust that kind of power to just anyone.

I'm reminded of my neighbor, a U.S. congressman who served twenty-five years in the United States Marine Corps. While serving under the authority of two presidents during his military career, he was responsible for carrying the nuclear "football"—the package containing launch codes for a nuclear attack. Imagine giving responsibility for the "button" that controls the U.S. nuclear arsenal to an unruly child! As long as we struggle against God's will and purpose like rebellious children insisting on our own way, we will never live in the power of the Spirit. We will never know how good and pleasing and perfect *His* will really is (Romans 12:2).

Sammy wanted it his way. His life was falling apart. A series of broken relationships, an attempted suicide, and a history of addiction and health problems finally brought him to his knees. He made his way into a local church and asked for a pastor.

The pastor on call had a heart for people like Sammy. For the first time in his life, he felt like somebody listened to him—really listened. Somebody cared. Sammy was a loner. He never let people get too close, because people couldn't be trusted. People let him down. He could only trust himself. And now, he found himself trusting this pastor. The pastor led him to Christ and mentored him. He introduced him to some good people. Sammy even met a nice woman and married her.

Things went okay for a while, until Sammy's marriage started to struggle. He didn't like his wife's overly righteous church friends, and he didn't like her spending time with them. He didn't like going to the church anymore. He didn't like the pastors, and he didn't like their messages. Sometimes they expected way too much of him! When people reached out to him, he shut them out. Besides, they were judging him. Who did they think they were, anyway? Sammy's marriage started breaking under the pressure. The fire burned hot as he battled old emotions and old habits. He really wanted to follow Jesus; he found comfort in knowing that someone bigger than himself was in charge of the universe. He wanted to live with the power of the Holy Spirit at his disposal. But he wanted to live life on *his* terms, not God's.

Sometimes our struggles can be a lot like Sammy's. We lay down our lives on the Lord's altar, and when His will clashes with our own, we grab it back again. If we truly want a personal relationship with Jesus, we must stop acting like rebellious children and put aside our own sinful desires. If we claim we belong to Him but continue to live for ourselves, the Lord can't fully trust us with the "button" that releases the powers of heaven and earth.

Jesus will always expose our deception. We can't follow Christ while we continue to follow the ways of the world. But if we surrender our will to God—if we leave ourselves on His altar—He will transform us into a new person by changing the way we think. Then, the desires of our hearts and minds will be perfectly aligned with His. Only then can He fully release His power (Romans 12:2). Only then can He trust us with the "button."

Today, you may be living in the furnace of suffering. But if you call yourself a Christ follower, your body is the temple of the Holy Spirit. He has given you a choice in how you will rule over your body, including all your thoughts and desires. When you truly lay down your life on the Lord's altar and pass the test of full surrender—when you lay aside your own selfish desires to follow Him—the Holy Spirit releases His power into you. He renews, reeducates, and redirects your mind to honor and serve God. Your life reflects His glorious presence, and everyone around you will bask in your glow. The Lord is your guide out of the fiery furnace. You move when the cloud moves. You stay when the cloud stays. You have become a living and holy sacrifice.

Heavenly Father, forgive me for my rebellion against you. Forgive me when I insist on my own way and for every time I take my life back into my own hands. Thank you for the gift of the Holy Spirit and the resurrection power that dwells within me. Lord, I want to come under your authority. More than anything, I want to live in fellowship with you. I want your heart and mind. Lord, I am your temple. Please fill me with your Holy Spirit. Transform me! Please lead me out of the furnace, Lord. Help me become a living and holy sacrifice, one that honors and serves you. In Jesus' name, amen.

LET SIN DIE

If your sinful nature controls your mind, there is death. But if the

Holy Spirit controls your mind, there is life and peace.

—ROMANS 8:6

The last thing I wanted to think about in the furnace of suffering was my "sinful nature." I knew Jesus died for my sins, but I wasn't always sure how that applied to me. *I'm not as bad as a lot of people I know*. It wasn't until cancer brought me to my knees that I finally understood *why* I needed a Savior. In the heat of the fire I poured myself into my Bible. I learned about my sinful human nature compared to the holiness and righteousness of a perfect God. We all fall short of His glorious standard, regardless of how "good" we are (Romans 3:23).

In His mercy, God restored my relationship with Him simply because I came to Him with a repentant heart. My rebellious sinful nature died with Christ on the cross (Romans 6:6). When I surrendered my life to Jesus, His grace set me free (Romans 6:14)! Gradually, through the fires of unemployment, broken relationships, loss, and grief, I learned He wants *all* of me. He wants my family and friends, my career and ambitions, my reputation, my possessions, my social life, and my daily schedule. Most important, He wants my will.

So I gave it all to Him. I am a new creation in Christ, a sinner saved by grace. I wake up to a brand-new day filled with God's peace, protected under the shelter of His wings. I'm invincible. And I have lots on my to-do list. Before I can settle into my morning devotions and my first cup of coffee, the phone rings. I'm needed at a meeting right away. It will only take a few minutes. Two hours later, I'm back in my office. I try to answer some urgent messages so I can get started on my writing, but my email isn't working. For twenty minutes I'm routed through my ISP's automated customer "service" system. I finally get a live body on the phone. An hour later, still no email. I try to be patient with the service technician who could use some serious public relations training. More phone calls. The doorbell rings. Everyone needs something from me, and they need it now. I have yet to write one word. My husband delivers the final blow. We have unexpected guests coming to stay. *Are you kidding? The house is a mess, we need groceries, and I have work to do!* My husband gets an earful of my built-up frustration. *This is not the morning I had planned.* It isn't even noon yet, and I'm having a full-blown melt-down!

Wait a minute. This isn't supposed to happen. My old sinful nature was crucified with Christ. I am a new creation—humble, pure, and devoted to God. I'm supposed to be *dead* to sin. When I accepted Jesus, I was set free from sin's power. I gave up my own plans, desires, or goals. I'm supposed to take joy in doing *His* will, not insist on my own way. Besides, I'm supposed to have the peace of Christ in me. Right now, I feel nothing that even remotely resembles peace. *What's wrong with me?*

Even the apostle Paul had his schizophrenic moments. His classic meltdown is recorded in Romans:

> I know I am rotten through and through so far as my old sinful nature is concerned. No matter which way I turn, I can't make myself do right. I want to, but I can't. When I want to do good, I don't. And when I try not to do wrong, I do it anyway. But if I

am doing what I don't want to do, I am not really the one doing it; the sin within me is doing it.

It seems to be a fact of life that when I want to do what is right, I inevitably do what is wrong. I love God's law with all my heart. But there is another law at work within me that is at war with my mind. This law wins the fight and makes me a slave to the sin that is still within me. Oh, what a miserable person I am! (Romans 7:18–24)

Oh, what a miserable person I am! I could have written this. Maybe you could have written this. One of the things I learned in the furnace is that being a believer does not eliminate sin from my life. It only took a moment of faith to surrender my life to Jesus. But to become *like* Jesus—to live a life that reflects His nature—takes a lifetime.

Paul compares his faith journey to a long and strenuous race (1 Corinthians 9:24–27). Our Lord knew we would struggle. That's why He sent a personal counselor, the Holy Spirit, to our rescue. The Holy Spirit and our sinful natures are constantly battling each other. We will never be free of this conflict (Galatians 5:17). We cannot fight our willful desires on our own strength. We must choose every day to surrender to God, and allow the Holy Spirit to control our minds and renew our thoughts and attitudes (Ephesians 4:22–24). When we have a meltdown and fall into sin, the Holy Spirit lovingly reaches down into our lives and picks us up again. His tender mercies start fresh every day (Lamentations 3:23).

God promised a life of joy, but we can never be completely redeemed from the fire and made whole in Christ until our hearts break over our sin. Sin is outright rebellion against God. Either sin wins the battle, or God wins. If you don't allow God to destroy the sin in your life, sin will destroy God's impact in your life. When you meet Him in the furnace, you come face-to-face with your own brokenness and His holiness.

Can you hear Him calling? *Come to me. Come just as you are.*

You step into His outstretched arms. He removes your sin as far away from you as the east is from the west (Psalm 103:12). His Spirit joins with yours. Each new day you make a conscious decision to let the Holy Spirit kill your worldly desires (Galatians 5:18). You don't worry when the meltdowns come and your peace flies out the window. There is no condemnation when you are in Him (Romans 8:1). You cry out with a repentant heart, and He reaches down into the fire to pick you up again. Gradually, all your ties with this world are broken. He has *all* of you. You emerge from the fire a new creation—humble, pure, and devoted to God. Your life reflects His because every day you let sin die.

Heavenly Father, forgive me for rebelling against you and letting my sinful nature control me. Lord, you know when I am miserable. You see every meltdown. You know how desperately I need a Savior! Thank you that I am a new creation and my old sinful nature died with you on the cross. Thank you for scattering my sins as far away from me as the east is from the west. Lord, I receive the gift of your Holy Spirit. I know that sin and Satan have no power over me unless I give them permission to influence me. I have no obligation whatsoever to follow my own sinful desires. Holy Spirit, I surrender my mind to you. Renew my thoughts and attitudes. Let my life reflect yours. Make me humble, pure, and devoted. Let my sin die every day. In Jesus' name, amen.

JUST DO IT!
THE OBEDIENCE TEST

*For God is working in you, giving you the desire to obey him
and the power to do what pleases him.*

—PHILIPPIANS 2:13

NO EXCUSE

Remember, it is sin to know what you ought to do

and then not do it.

—JAMES 4:17

Like any parent, God expects His children to obey everything exactly as He tells us. I don't know about you, but I can come up with lots of excuses for disobedience. *Can't you see my life is a mess? I have my own fire to fight! I'm too busy to be bothered with such things right now. I'll do it later. And when I do, I'll do it differently! I'd like to help out, but someone more qualified can take care of it. I really can't afford to get involved. I know I should tell my family and friends about my faith, but what will they think?*

God has never been impressed with our excuses. The Israelites wandered the desert for forty years as punishment for their countless acts of disobedience. Moses could barely get God's laws for righteous living down from the mountain before the people disobeyed the first commandment and worshiped a golden calf (Exodus 32:7–8). They rebelled against their leaders, demanded what they didn't have, and refused to follow God into the Promised Land (Numbers 11:4, 14:1–4, 16:3). Only their descendents and Caleb and Joshua made it to their final destination.

Even Moses didn't make it. After thirty-seven years of wandering, the next generation continued to whine like their parents. They accused Moses of bringing them out into the wilderness to die when they came to a place where there was no water to drink. God told Moses to speak to the rock to bring forth water so all the people could see His power and believe that He was still going to provide for their every need. It was supposed to be a faith-building opportunity. But Moses was fed up with their incessant nagging, and he did something foolish and out of character. In his anger he disobeyed God's direct order and dishonored Him before the people. He struck the rock twice with his staff and took credit for the water that poured out. Because of this, he was forbidden from entering the Promised Land (Numbers 20:2–12). God only allowed him to view it from a distance (Deuteronomy 34:1–4).

King Saul also learned the consequences of blatant disobedience. According to Old Testament law, only the priests could offer sacrifices to God. It was customary to offer a sacrifice to God before a crucial battle. As a vast army of Philistines approached and his own army scattered in fear, Saul grew impatient waiting for Samuel the priest to arrive. So he took matters into his own hands and offered the pre-battle sacrifice himself. When Samuel arrived, he had bad news for Saul—this act of rebellion was going to cost him his throne. God had chosen another to replace him as king (1 Samuel 13:8–14).

The prophet Jonah should have obeyed God the first time around. The Assyrians were Israel's greatest enemy, and Jonah hated them. When God told him to go to the capital city of Nineveh and warn the people of the Lord's judgment against them, Jonah boarded a ship heading in the opposite direction (Jonah 1:1–3). But Jonah couldn't escape from God or His assignment. God caused a violent storm in the region where his ship was sailing. Since he knew that he was responsible for it, he persuaded his reluctant crew members to throw him overboard in an attempt to calm the seas. When they did the storm immediately subsided, and Jonah was swallowed by a great fish (Jonah 1:4–17). After three days and three nights inside the fish's belly, God heard Jonah's prayer and rescued him. He gave Jonah a second chance, and this time he obeyed. He went to Nineveh and preached God's message in the streets. As a result of Jonah's obedience, the people repented and were delivered from God's judgment (Jonah 3:5–10).

What about today? Does God still speak in an audible voice like He did to Moses and the prophets? Sometimes. But He usually tells us what to do through a still, small voice in our spirit. Just ask Howie. After nearly fourteen months of unemployment, Howie and God were having regular conversations. When a recruiter called with a less-than-ideal opportunity, he took the weekend to think it over. Monday morning he announced he would not apply for the job.

Moments later, in his office, Howie heard a clear voice deep in his spirit. *Yes, you will.* So he obeyed God's prompting and eventually accepted the position, even though it defied his common sense. Over the next two years, no other opportunity surfaced. His career started over with God in the center. Today, he leads a ministry for the unemployed, counseling, mentoring, and praying with job seekers. God blessed his obedience. Eventually, He restored Howie's career and finances, but not before restoring his relationship with Jesus.

I heard God's voice too. But like Jonah, I ran in the other direction. Several years ago a friend died from an aggressive cancer. Many times in the last few months of her life, God prompted me to go see her. I had lots of excuses for not going to Nineveh, so I didn't. I suspect my own journey through cancer was a little like being in the belly of a fish. I don't know if God sent me there, but I do know He sent me back to Nineveh. This time, I was obedient. Today, I counsel, mentor, and pray with people suffering from all types of cancer. God, in His mercy, reached down into my fire and restored my health. He gave me a second chance to participate in His work, but not before restoring my relationship with Him, not before I learned obedience.

We may struggle to understand God in our suffering, but it's no great mystery what we should and shouldn't do (Deuteronomy 30:11). God speaks into our spirits and makes His will known to us in the Scriptures. All Scripture is God-inspired. God uses it to prepare and equip us for everything He wants us to do (2 Timothy 3:16–17). And His commands are very clear.

We're disobedient when we know what to do and don't do it. We're disobedient when we allow the concerns of this world to distract us from His leading (Matthew 8:21). We're disobedient when we have good intentions but we fail to act (Matthew 21:28–31). We're disobedient when we substitute our own good works for His clear directions (1 Samuel 15:22). As you read His Word and listen to His voice, He may ask you to do things you don't want to do. He may want you to share the Good News with others. He may want you to care for the sick, help the needy, forgive an enemy, or serve Him in a way that's way out of your comfort zone. He may send you to Nineveh.

Are you running out of excuses? If God seems far away and your fire rages on with no end in sight, He may be waiting for your obedience. God's next move often depends on how we respond to His commands. When we obey His word and His promptings, He reveals more of himself and gives us a deeper understanding of His ways (Matthew 25:23). When we disobey, He may remain silent. If you're still wondering what He wants you to do, nurture your prayer life and keep your Bible open. The next time He prompts you to do something, do it! The more you obey, the more He speaks to you, and the clearer His will and His nature becomes. Don't worry if you've whined, procrastinated, or jumped on a ship going in the opposite direction. He is a God of second chances. He is merciful and forgiving; He loves you even when you disappoint Him. He wants your obedience, and you have no excuse.

Heavenly Father, forgive me when I know what to do and I don't do it. Forgive me for making excuses for my disobedience. I'm sorry for the times I've complained, procrastinated, and allowed my own problems to distract me from your leading. I'm sorry for running in the other direction when you call me to do something. Thank you, Lord, for your Word, your Holy Spirit, and second chances. Lord, I want to hear your still, small voice. Help me clearly discern what you would have me do. Show me the areas of my life where I am disobedient to your will. Please give me boldness and courage to obey you without excuse. In Jesus' name, amen.

LAY DOWN YOUR ISAAC

Take your son, your only son—yes, Isaac,

whom you love so much—and go to the land of Moriah.

Sacrifice him there as a burnt offering on

one of the mountains, which I will point out to you.

—GENESIS 22:2

Imagine what Abraham was thinking. *Lay down my Isaac and sacrifice him as a burnt offering? Are you serious? The child I love?* If you were Abraham, what would you do? After the initial shock, I'd probably argue with God. Maybe I'd ask some trusted friends what they thought. Maybe I'd refuse. But Abraham didn't refuse. He didn't call a meeting to ask all his friends what they thought he should do. He didn't let his own human reasoning or emotions interfere with his obedience. He didn't hesitate. He obeyed immediately. But then, Abraham had plenty of opportunities to learn obedience. He obeyed God's instructions for thirty years before he carried out one of the greatest acts of obedience in history.

During this time of training, Abraham learned many hard lessons that deepened his character and his understanding of God. He learned to trust God's nature and obey without question. First, God told him to pick up stakes and travel to a new land (Genesis 12:1). Abraham chose obedience over the comfort of his present situation. God continued to test him as he wandered in Canaan, battled kings, interceded for Sodom and Gomorrah, and waited years for a son.

In this ultimate test, God told him to sacrifice his beloved son, Isaac. Abraham trusted God's provision and carried out His instructions (Genesis 22:8). He knew it was inconsistent with God's character to allow the sacrifice to take place. Yet he was willing to carry out the command. Sure enough, at the last minute, God sent an angel who told Abraham to lay down the knife. "Do not hurt the boy in any way, for now I know that you truly fear God. You have not withheld even your beloved son from me" (Genesis 22:12). Abraham's descendants and all the nations of the earth were blessed abundantly because Abraham obeyed God (Genesis 22:16–18).

Abraham had reached a level of obedience where he would do absolutely anything for God. Sometimes I wonder if I'll ever get to that place in my faith journey. Sometimes it just feels like God expects way too much of me. But then I remember: He is God. When He grabs hold of our hearts, we don't get to decide where He will take us or how far He will ask us to go. We can't draw a line in the sand and tell the Lord we will follow Him *this* far, and no farther. No, He wants *all* of us (Romans 12:1–2).

God isn't asking us to give up things just for the sake of denying ourselves. He wants us to be willing to give up, *in our hearts,* anything that stands in the way of having a full life in Him. He wants to sever the ties to all the things that bind us to this world. He wants nothing to stand between our relationship with Him, whether it's our possessions, financial security, health, strength and abilities, or even the people we love.

Does it feel as if God has asked you to lay down your *Isaac*? Perhaps you've lost your job or your business. Maybe you're facing a life-threatening disease or your spouse has left for good. A child is in serious trouble. Your home is destroyed in a hurricane, along with your job and your entire city. You've lost someone dear to you. The stool crumbles beneath you. You cry out to God for healing. You pray for restoration. You beg Him for a job or a solution to your financial crisis. You pray for enough courage to face the next day.

Lord, what more could you possibly want from me? Do you want my Isaac too? No, God doesn't want your Isaac. He wants to give you what you need most. He wants to give you Jesus. He wants your intimate knowledge of His Word and His character to become your underlying foundation for living. He wants your obedience. He wants your heart. He wants you to love Him more than any activity, achievement, or relationship. He wants you to be totally and passionately sold out because your relationship with Him is the only thing that really matters. It's the only thing you have that can never be destroyed (Hebrews 12:27–28).

In your fire today, maybe you're tempted to argue with God. *But Lord, I could never be like Abraham!* Thankfully, God doesn't expect this level of commitment and obedience from us all at once. Our life on this earth is a grueling training ground to become like Jesus (1 Corinthians 9:24–27). God gradually changes us from the inside out.

Sometimes we get it backwards. We think we have to change outwardly first in order to be worthy of coming into a relationship with God. But God does all the work. He changes our hearts to be more like His. All we have to do is *be available*. All we have to do is let God purify us like He purified Abraham—step by step through obedience.

Don't worry; He'll start with the small things. He may prompt you to find a church home, ask for prayer, or pray for a friend. He may ask you to make a change in your lifestyle. When you obey immediately, God will develop your character for greater tests. He'll keep testing you until your purpose and His purpose are one and the same—until your mind resembles His and you become a mirror that brightly reflects His glory (2 Corinthians 3:18). With each passed test of obedience will come a greater love for God and a deeper understanding of His character. Someday, if He asks you to lay down your Isaac, you'll be ready.

Heavenly Father, forgive me for holding on so tightly to the things of this world. I'm sorry for the times when I don't follow you as far as you want to take me. Lord, thank you that my relationship with you is the one thing in my life that can never be destroyed. Thank you for your patience and grace when I fall short. Lord, I want to be like your servant Abraham. I want to be totally sold out in my love and obedience to you. Help me get to a place where I can obey you without question or hesitation. Please give me strength, courage, and wisdom to follow you step by step. In Jesus' name, amen.

CERTAIN OF GOD

How can we understand the road we travel?

It is the Lord who directs our steps.

—PROVERBS 20:24

Nicky had the perfect plan. She married her college sweetheart at twenty-four and they both started successful careers. They worked hard and saved enough money to buy a nice three-bedroom house in the suburbs. She wanted to start a family at age twenty-seven and be done by age thirty. She planned to have two children. A boy and a girl would be perfect, but if she had two boys or two girls, she would consider having three. She would go off the Pill and be pregnant by Christmas. Christmas came and went. The next Christmas passed, and the next. Tests, doctor visits, more tests, and frequent disappointment filled the time in between. Nicky didn't plan on infertility.

Jack was a natural-born leader. At least, people always told him so. He had a successful career in senior management and a good family. Now he had found the perfect church home. His wife joined a women's Bible study, and the kids quickly adapted to the youth programs. He and his wife took classes, volunteered regularly, and became small-group leaders. Jack could immediately see ways to improve how the church was managed. He knew his leadership and administrative gifts were a perfect fit for the church council, and perhaps in the future, for the role of council president. He was convinced God had brought him to this church for this specific purpose. Jack was nominated for an open position on the council and went through an extensive interviewing process, where he shared his credentials and his improvement strategies with various members of the selection committee. He was stunned when a "lesser-qualified" candidate was elected to the council instead.

Robert didn't like his job. He didn't like his boss or his co-workers. He didn't even like the customers anymore. It was probably a good thing because the company wasn't doing so well. There was talk of downsizing. He was tired of sales, but it was the only type of work he'd ever done. At the close of this quarter's business, he vowed he would get ahead of the inevitable and start looking for a new position. Only problem was, he had no idea what he wanted to do or for whom he wanted to do it. He started going to a job-transition group at his local church. For weeks, he prayed for God to reveal His plan and His purposes for his life. He prayed for God to show him clearly what his next career move should be. He prayed and prayed. God was silent as Robert grew more frustrated with each passing day.

What are your goals for the next five years? What is your ten-year plan? What are your plans for retirement? Our natural tendency is to forecast and plan. If we need help, we can engage the expert services of financial planners, career planners, and life planners. Often, we're a lot like Jack. We come up with our own elaborate plans and assume we have God's blessing. Or we can be like Nicky and leave Him out of our planning altogether. Unfortunately, the best-laid plans lead to disappointment when our expectations aren't met. And our plans will always fall short of our expectations if we leave God out of the picture. We will always be disappointed if we strive on our own power to reach our goals, even if our goals are God-ordained. His timing is perfect. He is sovereign over our past, present, and future, so it's pointless to plan without Him. Maybe you've noticed how easily He can step in and rearrange things! It's wise to plan ahead, but we always need to keep God in the center. And we shouldn't be too surprised when He draws us off course. He might take us on a little side trip to teach us obedience, build our faith, and reveal more of His character. Sometimes He simply has a better idea. His plans are always bigger and more exciting than any we could dream up on our own (Isaiah 55:8–9).

As believers, we often find ourselves like Robert—clueless about what God is up to. We desperately want Him to uncover His divine plan for our lives, or at least show us the next chapter. We want answers. In our earthly lives, we will always live in the uncertainty of our circumstances. We will never be certain what God is up to or what He will do next. But we can always be certain of God. When we walk closely with Him, our lives will be full of joyful spontaneity and expectancy. His plan will only be revealed in *His* appointed time and *His* appointed way, not ours.

We want so desperately to know exactly where we're going and how we're going to get there. We want God to light up the whole road and reveal all the answers to our questions. But He wants to reveal himself instead. He does it through obedience. Step by step, He orders our way. With each step He lights the path under our feet. When we obey, He lights the next step. And He delights in every detail of our journey. We might stumble along the way or stray off-course, but we will not fall far from His path (Psalm 37:23). He's given us His Word to guide and protect us (Psalm 119:133).

One thing is certain. You didn't plan your fire. This wasn't a side trip you intended to take. Sometimes the road God leads us down makes absolutely no sense at the time (Proverbs 20:24). You won't see how God was working until years later, when you look back. You don't need to know why He took you to this hot and dismal place. You just need to trust He knows what He's doing. When your heavenly Father looks into your fire, even your most sophisticated plans are like the plans of a child to Him. He has so much more for you—plans for good and not disaster, to give you a future and a hope (Jeremiah 29:11)!

But the joy of knowing Him is in the journey, not the destination. Little by little you discover His plan for your life through the daily process of obedience. So start every day with a willing heart. Ask Him to show you what exciting thing He has planned for you today. Then open your Bible and listen for His still, small voice. When He lights the step under your feet, be obedient to His guidance. Do the same tomorrow . . . and the next day . . . and the next. You may never know for certain where the road is leading, but you can be certain of God.

Heavenly Father, forgive me for leaving you out of my plans and for striving to get ahead of you and your perfect timing. Forgive me for not trusting that you know what's best for me. Lord, I know you have a perfect plan for my life. Thank you for the delightful side trips that teach me obedience and help me know you better. Thank you that I can be certain of you in a world of uncertainty. Lord, please give me a willing heart. Help me to obey you as step by step you light the path under my feet today. Help me to give up the need to know where the road is leading. My future rests in your hands. In Jesus' name, amen.

Shed Your Pride Coats

So humble yourselves under the mighty power of God,

and in his good time he will honor you.

—1 Peter 5:6

Joseph was born when Jacob, his father, was an old man. Jacob loved him more than any of his other children, so he gave Joseph a beautiful, colorful robe as a special gift. The robe became a symbol of his father's favoritism, and his brothers deeply resented it. It could have also been a symbol of Joseph's youthful pride. When he had a prophetic dream that he would rule over all his household, he flaunted his favored position and bragged about it. His brothers were so enraged that they plotted to kill him and eventually sold him into slavery when he was seventeen years old.

During his thirteen years as a slave and prisoner in Egypt, Joseph encountered one trial after another. He faced sexual temptation, was falsely accused and punished for doing the right thing, and was long forgotten in prison by those he helped. Through it all, he developed strong character and deep wisdom. His positive response transformed each test of the fire into a new opportunity for him. The Pharaoh was so impressed with Joseph's personal integrity and spiritual ability to interpret dreams that he made Joseph the second in command over the entire nation when he was only thirty years old.

God used the evil actions of Joseph's brothers to fulfill His plan for both Joseph and the Hebrew nation. As ruler, Joseph controlled the food supply that saved his relatives and all of Egypt from famine. And in the unfolding circumstances, he paved the way for the next step in Israel's destiny (Genesis 37–47). Whether he was in the pit of despair or ruler of the land, Joseph faithfully obeyed God. Each fiery trial brought him to a place of deep humility. Joseph shed his coat of pride, and God exalted him.

A few years ago I wore my own pride coat. I had my act together. I had a great family and a successful consulting business. Everything was on track, and I owed it all to my skills, intelligence, business savvy, and a lot of hard work. I knew how to stand on my own two feet, and I didn't need any help or advice from anyone.

I even had God figured out. I went to church on Sunday, listened to the sermons, and thought I understood everything about Him. I wasn't even close to understanding. When cancer took my life off track, my skills, intelligence, and business savvy were useless. All I had was God, and He had plenty more to teach me. Doctors, tests, chemotherapy, and an uncertain future left me bald and broken on the bathroom floor—stripped of every hair and pride coat, humbled before God. I like to think God used this time to develop my character. I like to think I learned something about obedience in this place of deep humility.

I like to think so, because pride can get us into a lot of trouble. It tempts us to do what we know isn't God-honoring and hinders us from being obedient to Him. The Bible is full of examples of the dangers of pride. Pride motivated Adam and Eve to disobey God and eat from the forbidden tree (Genesis 3:1–6). It led Cain to murder his brother (Genesis 4:5–8). It drove King Saul to hunt down David (1 Samuel 18:8). It was at the core of the Pharisees' hatred toward Jesus and led His disciples to argue over their place in His kingdom (Luke 9:46). Pride can keep us from forgiving someone who offends us. It can cause us to strive for status and power. It can keep us from leaving a sinful lifestyle or allowing ourselves to be corrected and held accountable by other believers. Pride can be the root of our disobedience, and it always goes before a fall (Proverbs 16:18).

When it comes to obedience, we can learn a lot from Jesus; He learned obedience through suffering (Hebrews 5:8). Just imagine for a moment. The God who created the universe—the God who set the stars in place and called them by name—this same God chose to leave the comforts of heaven to come down to earth in human form. Though He was God, He did not cling to His rights as God. He made himself nothing and took the humble position of a slave (Philippians 2:5–7). He walked with us, lived with us, ate with us, and suffered with us. He never uttered a word while He was scorned, tortured, and mocked by His enemies. In the ultimate act of humility, He was obedient unto death (Philippians 2:8). His obedience gave us direct access to the throne room of God. God honored His Son by exalting Him to the highest position in heaven and earth.

Jesus often reminded His followers that whoever lifts himself up will be humbled, and whoever humbles himself will be lifted up (Matthew 23:12). A wise friend drove this point home to me in another way. She had me imagine the voice of God speaking directly to me. *My job is to lift you up, and your job is to humble yourself. If you continue to do my job, I'll have to continue to do yours.* Her words were hard to hear. But they always remind me to stay humble and aware of my total dependence on God, especially during those tough times when He is refining my character and teaching me obedience through my suffering.

Are you still trying to do His job? Are you wearing any pride coats? Maybe you've been depending on your own strength for too long. Maybe you've been striving for status and power or seeking recognition. Maybe you've isolated yourself. You're reluctant to ask for help or unwilling to receive teaching or correction. Your friends and neighbors may be impressed with all your success, but God cares more about your humility. When you achieve greatness in the world's eyes—when you lift yourself up—you get the credit. But when you humble yourself and *He* lifts you up, He gets the glory. You become His witness and the world sees all He has done for you. Maybe today finds you on your knees in a bald and broken place in the middle of the fire. You've been falsely accused, treated unjustly, and long forgotten. Today, it's just you and God. Don't be troubled; He hasn't forgotten you. Do your job and let Him do His. When He looks into your heart and sees you shed your pride coats, He *will* honor you.

Heavenly Father, forgive me for the pride coats that keep me from obeying you. I'm so sorry for taking over your job. Forgive me for exalting myself instead of letting you lift me up. Thank you for the ultimate obedience of your Son that gives me eternal life and the awesome privilege of coming to you in prayer. Please use my time in the fire to reveal the areas in my life where I've been disobedient. Lord, I humble myself before you. Help me to shed my pride coats. Let the world see what you have done in me. Let my life bring you glory! In Jesus' name, amen.

Because You Love Him

Those who obey my commandments are the ones who love me.
And because they love me, my Father will love them, and I will
love them. And I will reveal myself to each one of them.

—John 14:21

My son, Bryan, played hockey. Like in any other competitive sport, a good coach will always get the best from the players. Tryouts are stressful because there are always more players than positions. After a week of vigorous tryouts during his junior year of high school, the coach chose him to be on the team. During practice and games, he taught my son to be the best hockey player he could be. When Bryan was obedient and listened to his coach, he earned praise and playing time. When he went his own way and didn't follow the coach's instructions, he was corrected and disciplined. Bryan knew his coach cared. The coach invested in him and believed in him. Throughout the season, the coach kept raising the bar and encouraging him to achieve his potential. As a result, he earned Bryan's respect and devotion. Bryan played his heart out. He followed the plan and did what he was told. He didn't want to let his coach down.

And so it is with your heavenly Father. Just as a good coach chooses his team, or an earthly parent chooses to love his child, God chose you (John 15:16). He loved you first, long before you knew Him. He died for you, rose again, and extended the invitation for you to join Him forever in eternity. You make the next choice—to accept and submit to His authority, or reject His divine offer so you can have it your way. He is your Lord and Master, the maker of heaven and earth. He *deserves* your obedience. But He will never insist on it or force you to give it to Him. He won't come barging into your fire, demanding your devotion. He wants it to come from your love for Him, not out of duty.

When you accept His invitation you become part of God's family; you're on *His* team. When you fall He'll pick you up again (Matthew 14:31). When you don't have the strength to go on He'll encourage you (Philippians 4:13). When you make a mistake His grace will cover you (1 Timothy 1:15–16). And when you go off on your own way and disobey His commands, the Bible says you will experience His divine discipline (Hebrews 12:5–6).

No one likes discipline. And the Lord's discipline can be very confusing. It's easy to wonder how this God who loves you with such reckless abandon can allow you to suffer at the same time. You might even wonder if God allowed your current fire to come into your life as a form of divine discipline. When I was diagnosed with cancer, I sure wondered. We may never know the answer. We do know that there are times when our heavenly Father may seem callous or indifferent. Sometimes, the Coach might sit us on the bench. When we can't see His face in the fire—when He seems distant—we can take comfort in knowing that ultimately, He will give us clear understanding and justify all that He has allowed in our lives.

When we do suffer from divine discipline, it is always a sign of our Lord's deep love for us. We shouldn't be discouraged when He corrects us. As we endure His discipline, God is treating us as His own children (Hebrews 12:6). Unlike our earthly fathers or a good coach who disciplines us to the best of their human abilities, the discipline of our heavenly Father is always perfect and right (Hebrews 12:9–10).

How we respond will determine whether our suffering bears fruit (Psalm 126:4–6; Genesis 41:52). We can be angry, feel sorry for ourselves, and never grow in our walk with Christ or fully realize His plan for us. Or we can ask God what He is trying to teach us. He is like a demanding coach who will push us to our limits, encouraging us to become all that we can be. He will refine or remove anything in our lives that keeps us from being obedient and experiencing abundant life in Him.

Yes, discipline is always painful, but God promises a quiet harvest of right living for those who are trained in this way (Hebrews 12:11). Just as following a good coach may lead to a state tournament title or the experience of victory, obedience to Jesus will lead you to places you never dreamed possible. You will experience the pain He feels for the lost and those held captive to sin. You will experience the joy He feels when the blind see and the lost are found. You will witness the sick healed, broken lives made whole again, people in bondage set free, and those who mourn receive comfort. You are part of His team; you get "playing time." You experience the awesome privilege of participating in the work of His kingdom. You are blessed beyond your wildest dreams . . . all because you obeyed your Coach.

You obeyed Him because you love Him, and you would never consider not obeying. Just as my son was devoted to his hockey coach, your genuine love for God becomes your motive for obedience. You don't want to let Him down. You don't follow the rules simply because you think you can gain something from it or because it makes you look good.

Obedience without love is nothing but legalism. God doesn't care about your showy sacrifices and your religious traditions. He cares about your heart (Isaiah 29:13; Matthew 15:8). Genuine obedience to God's commands is the true test of your heart; it will always be your greatest motivation for serving Him. And because you've learned true obedience, He will reveal all He has in store for you. He'll take you from one victory to another. You're on His winning team. All because you love Him.

Heavenly Father, forgive me when I rebel against your divine discipline and stray from your plan. I'm sorry for resisting when you push me to my limit to help me grow. Lord, thank you for choosing me to be on your team. Thank you for encouraging me, for picking me up when I fall, and for giving me the strength to go on. Thank you for your grace that covers me when I make mistakes. Lord, I don't want to disappoint you. Please let my genuine love for you become my true motivation for obedience. Show me the areas of my life where my obedience falls short or is not from my heart. Lord, I want playing time! Please let me experience victory in you! In Jesus' name, amen.

Sing Hallelujah Anyway

The Joy Test

Whatever happens, dear brothers and sisters,

may the Lord give you joy.

—Philippians 3:1

Rejoice!

Always be full of joy in the Lord. I say it again—rejoice!

—Philippians 4:4

Do you ever feel you're just one "if only" away from true happiness? If only that promotion would go through, you could get your career on the right track. If only you had a different boss. If only you could get a decent raise. If only your workload would lighten up. If only you could find a job. If only you could have children. If only your kids could stay out of trouble. If only they were happy. If only your spouse would listen to you. If only the weather would warm up. If only you could go on vacation. If only you had a bigger house in a better neighborhood. If only you had more time. If only you had more money. If only you had more friends. If only you had better health. If only life was perfect. *Then* you could be happy.

Unfortunately, life on this earth isn't perfect. It's filled with circumstances and events we can't control, and expectations others can never meet. Sometimes life is good. We're on top of the mountain. Everything seems to be going our way. Then suddenly, with no warning, everything collapses, and we find ourselves in the valley of despair. A business goes under or a career is side-tracked. A relationship crumbles. We face a serious health crisis or a devastating loss. People disappoint us and expectations fall short. When our joy is dependent on external circumstances, our emotions run the gamut from the highest peaks to the lowest valleys from one situation to the next.

The apostle Paul experienced the thrill of spreading the Good News, working miracles, and founding churches throughout the Roman Empire. But he also experienced great suffering, persecution, and opposition to his ministry. On their missionary journey to Macedonia, Paul and Silas were stripped, severely beaten, and placed in stocks in a cold, dark prison cell. They could have compiled a long list of "if onlys." *If only the guards would loosen our chains. If only they would move us out of the inner dungeon. If only the city officials would let us go. . . .*

Instead, they prayed and sang hymns to God while the other prisoners listened. God caused a great earthquake that released them from their chains, but not before they demonstrated the true source of their joy (Acts 16:22–26). Not even the most painful trial could steal the joy that came from the Holy Spirit living within them. During his ministry, Paul learned to be content in every situation, whether extreme poverty or abundant wealth, full stomach or empty, physical pain, or imprisonment. His secret? He knew Jesus was the source of his strength (Philippians 4:11–13). Whether he found himself on the top of the mountain or in the deepest valley, Paul knew Jesus was always with him.

Over six hundred years earlier, the prophet Habakkuk looked around at the violence and corruption in the land, and his heart was broken. It was shortly before Babylon conquered Judah, and he knew disaster was coming. Habakkuk decided his feelings would not be controlled by the likelihood of barren fields and empty barns, but by God's promise to give him strength. He would rejoice in the Lord, even if the fig trees had no blossoms, the vines had no grapes, the olive crops failed, and the flocks died in the fields (Habakkuk 3:17–18). He could not control his circumstances or the impending disaster, but he could control his response. He chose to look past his worldly concerns and praise the Lord, even if everything that mattered to him collapsed. He rejoiced because he knew his Lord would give him strength and joy during the tough times to come.

What about you? Will you allow your fiery trials to steal your joy? With each passing day, you long for your circumstances to change. As you battle the flames, you might compile a long list of "if onlys." Or you might discover the secret of true joy.

True joy doesn't depend on your outward circumstances. It doesn't depend on whether God satisfies every longing, releases your chains, and rescues you from the fire. It comes from your relationship with Jesus. It comes from knowing He loves you, lives in you, and has completely wiped away your sins. It comes from an unwavering hope in His gift of salvation. It comes from knowing that *you* are His precious child, and in Him the highest peaks and the lowest valleys are all the same. Let His spirit fill you so full that no empty barn, no barren field, no amount of poverty or pain, no chains or dark prisons can ever steal your joy. Rejoice and always be full of joy in the Lord! I say it again—rejoice!

Heavenly Father, forgive me for depending on my external circumstances for the source of my joy. Thank you, Lord, that I am your precious child and your Holy Spirit lives in me. Thank you for your strength when times are tough. Lord, I know my happiness doesn't depend on the "happenings" in my life. True joy depends on my relationship with you. Help me to praise you from the middle of the fire! Help me experience the joy of your presence and the joy of my salvation. Help me to rejoice in you from the highest peaks and the lowest valleys! In Jesus' name, amen.

Joy Overflowing

I have told you this so that you will be filled with my joy.

Yes, your joy will overflow!

—John 15:11

Mark called the family across the street the Smiley Faced Church People. He was going through a tough time, and they reached out to help his family with groceries, transportation, and other basic needs. It seemed they were always helping someone. Kids loved to play at their house. *His* kids loved to play at their house. Now his own wife had joined their weekly Bible study and was even going to church with them on Sundays. He couldn't understand why they cared about his family. Didn't they think he could handle his own affairs? It just wasn't normal to be so friendly, especially when he gave them no reason to be friendly. As annoyed as he was, there was something about them. . . . He couldn't quite put his finger on it, but deep down inside, Mark wanted what they had.

What *did* they have? The disciples got a taste of their secret before Jesus completed His earthly mission. He gathered them together for a little talk so they would know what to expect after His arrest and death. But first, He washed their feet. He wanted to show them that serving others was the path of blessing (John 13:4–5, 12–17). Over supper, He promised to send the Holy Spirit to guide, comfort, and counsel them after He ascended into heaven. The Holy Spirit would live within them, never abandon them, and give them a deep and everlasting peace (John 14:15–18, 27).

Jesus warned them of the sorrow they would feel over the events to come, but gave them encouraging news. No one would be able to steal the joy they would have when they would see Him again (John 16:22)! After His mission was successfully completed, they could go directly to the Father and ask for anything in Jesus' name. They would not only receive what they asked for but also experience abundant joy (John 16:23–24). But the only way they could have this personal relationship with the Father was through Him (John 14:6). He promised He would prepare a special room for each of them in His Father's eternal mansion and come back to get them when everything was ready (John 14:2–3).

Jesus told His disciples all these things so they would be filled with joy (John 17:13). And this same joy He left with them belongs to us. He was handed over to His enemies as a love offering for our sin. When we accept Him as our Lord and Savior, He forgives us and makes us right with God (2 Corinthians 5:21). As God's children, we are joint heirs with Christ to *all* His treasures (Romans 8:16–17). We were once helpless victims of death, but now death has no victory over us (1 Corinthians 15:55–58). We were once doomed by our sinful nature, but now we have a new life in Christ (Romans 6:4).

Now *that's* cause for celebration! No wonder those church people wore smiles on their faces. Jesus came to give us an abundant life (John 10:10), and when He said *abundant,* He meant abundant—a life overflowing with love, peace, patience, kindness, goodness, faithfulness, gentleness, self-control, and *joy* (Galatians 5:22–24). Your Lord is a very generous giver. The true secret of joy is maintaining intimate contact with the Giver of Life.

Jesus used a grapevine to describe this relationship. He is the vine, and you are a branch. If you stay in fellowship with Him like a branch stays connected to a vine, you will remain vital, healthy, and fruitful. You bask in His love, your prayers are answered, and your joy overflows. But if you get separated from Christ, you can do nothing (John 15:5–11). You will never achieve joy on your own power any more than a branch can survive when it's cut off from the vine. He is the source of your life-giving power. When you are connected to your Life Source, His life and your life are one; His divine nature passes into yours. All the joy that is *His* becomes yours.

Eventually, Mark discovered the secret of the Smiley Faced Church People. In fact, he became one of them. He discovered Jesus. He learned that spending quiet time every day in the Bible and praying is the only way to stay connected with Him. It sounds easy enough. But the world will always try to distract you from spending time with God. You might make a point to get up early and read your Bible, but your morning turns to chaos. You might set aside time for Bible study and prayer over lunch, and an unexpected crisis steals your noon hour. You might plan to catch up with God after supper, but instead you run to a meeting, catch up on household chores, and help the kids with their homework. You crawl into bed determined to pray, and you can't stay awake. The day is over. Without even realizing it, you've cut yourself off from your Life Source. And without regular spiritual nourishment, true joy will always be a wistful, elusive goal.

Even those Smiley Faced Church People have to work at staying connected with Jesus. You can too. Make it a regular habit to sit at His feet, study His word, and live out His teachings in your daily life. Make abiding in Him so familiar that you instantly know when you've stepped out of His presence. Then, when the stresses and strains of this world begin to steal your joy, stop instantly and find a quiet place where you can commune with your Father. Come back into the calm. Rest in His secret place, under the shadow of the Almighty, where no power on earth can find you (Psalm 91:1). Let His divine nature flow through you, because the joy of the Spirit is unlike any happiness you will ever know. It's a deep unwavering joy that comes from a personal relationship with the Father—a joy so grounded in Jesus that no circumstance could ever shake it. It's an overflowing joy that puts a smile on your face.

Heavenly Father, forgive me for not spending more time with you. You are the source of abundant life, the true source of my joy! Lord, thank you for the Holy Sprit that lives within me and gives me a deep everlasting peace. Father, I know the only way I can come to you is through your Son. Thank you for the new life I have in you! Lord, you are the vine and I am the branch. I know I can do nothing apart from you. Help me stay connected to my Life Source. Help me resist the daily distractions that would keep me from spending time with you. I know that in your presence I am complete—vital, healthy, fruitful, and joy filled. In Jesus' name, amen.

CAST YOUR CARES

Give all your worries and cares to God,

for he cares about what happens to you.

—1 PETER 5:7

Ed was a natural-born worrier. He was also a high-achieving type A perfectionist. Over the years he learned that the best way to cope with his worry was to *take charge*. And take charge he did— on all fronts. His family never worried about a thing because Ed was in charge of all the finances, schedules, discipline, motorized toys, and the beautiful home he had built for them in heart of the suburbs. His church never worried about a thing either, because Ed was in charge of the finances, the budget, and the capital campaign. The civic organizations he served had it easy, because Ed was in charge of the fund-raisers and the community events. Even his direct reports didn't worry. When their company was sold, Ed simply started his own company and hired them all. No one worried when Ed was around, because Ed worried for them.

But something was missing. Ed felt no joy in his success. He felt overwhelmed. Sometimes he felt like a hockey goalie: The pucks came flying at him at lightning speed, and his job was to let nothing get past him into the net. The pucks flew faster and faster when his company started having cash-flow problems, but Ed just worked harder and harder. Worry began to suffocate him when his best efforts failed to improve the situation.

In desperation, he started borrowing from some of the accounts he managed. He planned to pay it back, but he kept falling further behind. He couldn't let his family down. He couldn't let his employees down. He couldn't let his church or community know he was in trouble. For the first time in Ed's life, the puck got past him. Worry turned to panic, and panic turned to hopelessness. He looked toward the future and could see no way out. An attempted suicide finally brought him to his knees.

A group of strong Christian men and a good Christian counselor came alongside Ed and showed him the love of Christ. For the first time in his life, God's mercy and grace became real and personal. He made restitution, downsized his lifestyle, and restructured his finances. His life started over with Jesus in the center. Through his healing and recovery, Ed learned that living a life of joy comes from sitting in the presence of God and experiencing perfect fellowship with Him.

How quickly the worries and cares of this world can pull us out of His presence and choke out our joy (Mark 4:19)! If our greatest desire is to keep up with other people and pursue wealth and nice things, we will always give too much thought to our circumstances, and not nearly enough thought to our relationship with Jesus. It's not too surprising to find our joy is gone and our burden is heavy. It gets heavier and heavier because we carry it alone.

Whenever we carry our burdens on our own shoulders, we are not fully trusting God. We are like oxen yoked to a harness, pulling a full load of worry on our own power. To tap into *His* strength, Jesus said we must take His yoke upon ourselves and learn from Him (Matthew 11:29). If we get beside Jesus, we pull the burden together and He carries the weight. His yoke fits us perfectly, and the burden He gives us is light (Matthew 11:29–30). It doesn't matter if the burden we pull is our own doing. Ed learned he could come to God with a repentant heart even when his struggles were caused by his own sin. We can give *all* our worries and cares to Jesus because He cares so deeply about what happens to us.

Yes, Jesus cares. He cares so much that He had some very strong words to say about worry. If you listen closely, you might hear Him speaking to you in the fire. *I am God, the Creator of heaven and earth, the God who created you. I saw you before you were born and laid out every minute of your life before a single day had passed* (Psalm 139:16). *Can worrying change your situation or add one single moment? Don't you think I can handle your problems? Don't you trust me? Do you think I ignore those who depend on me? I feed the birds and dress the lilies in beautiful splendor, and they do nothing to earn their keep. Aren't you far more valuable to me than birds and flowers? Don't fret about the everyday concerns of life. I already know what you need. Focus on me, and make my kingdom your first concern. I will help you with today's burden. Don't weigh yourself down with the burdens of yesterday and the uncertainties of tomorrow. Yesterday's burdens are long forgotten and tomorrow will bring its own worries* (Matthew 6:25–34).

Are you convinced? Even your best intentions can get sidetracked. When the cares of this world pull you out of His presence and threaten to choke your joy, stop and pray (Philippians 4:6). Let every single worry, whether it's marriage, children, work, health, money, or relationships, be your cue to come humbly into His presence and acknowledge your need for Him. When you pray with a thankful heart and tell Him what you need, He'll cover you with a peace that surpasses all human understanding (Philippians 4:7).

God's peace is not like the peace of this world (John 14:27); it doesn't come from good feelings or positive thinking. It comes from knowing that God is in control of your circumstances. It's a peace that flows like a river through a dry and desolate wilderness. In the midst of the hottest fire, you can be like a well-watered tree on the riverbank—untouched by worries of heat and drought—

that is strong and fruitful in the midst of crisis (Jeremiah 17:7–8).

When the Spirit of God lives within you, you're invincible. No power in heaven or earth is strong enough to steal your joy. You're like that strong, fruitful tree that cannot be moved. The joy of the Lord *is* your strength (Nehemiah 8:10). Whatever worries you today, it's probably disrupting your relationships, hindering your productivity, damaging your health, and standing in the way of your relationship with God. It's your cue to lighten your load. Come humbly into His presence and let His power flow through you. Cast your cares on Jesus and experience the joy.

Heavenly Father, forgive me when I carry the burdens of everyday life on my own shoulders. I'm sorry for not trusting you to meet my needs. Forgive me for letting the cares of this world pull me out of your presence and steal my joy. Lord, thank you for carrying the weight of my sin and all my burdens on your shoulders. Lord, you know everything about me and I have no need you can't supply. Help me make my relationship with you my primary concern. Help me focus just on today, not the burdens of yesterday or the uncertainties of tomorrow. Lord, today I cast my cares and worries on you. Come, Holy Spirit; let me experience the joy of your presence! In Jesus' name, amen.

No Fear

So we will not fear, even if earthquakes come

and the mountains crumble into the sea.

—Psalm 46:2

After Jesus fed the five thousand, He went up to the hills to pray while His disciples hopped a boat back to Bethsaida. During the night, a strong wind rose while they were far from land in the middle of the lake. They struggled desperately to row against the heavy waves. About three o'clock in the morning Jesus noticed they were in trouble. He could have calmed the wind and the waves from the shore, but instead, He came to them walking on the water. When the disciples saw Him they screamed in terror. They were sure He was a ghost. But Jesus spoke to their fears. "It's all right," he said. "I am here! Don't be afraid" (Matthew 14:27).

Peter, known for his impulsive nature, immediately called out to Him, " 'Lord, if it's really you, tell me to come to you by walking on water.' 'All right, come,' Jesus said" (Matthew 14:28–29). Without a moment's hesitation, Peter jumped over the side of the boat and walked toward Jesus. Imagine his joy! He's walking on the water's surface in the middle of the lake, and he's not sinking! He was so faith-filled and connected to his Lord that he even shared His power over the natural realm. But his joy quickly left him as he started noticing the high waves crashing around him. Suddenly, he was terrified and began to sink. " 'Save me, Lord!' he shouted. Instantly Jesus reached out his hand and grabbed him" (Matthew 14:30–31).

I know exactly how Peter felt. Once I got over the initial shock of a cancer diagnosis, I planted my eyes firmly on Jesus. Where else could I turn when the storm was raging and my life was on the line? I was so faith-filled and connected to the power of God, I'm pretty sure I was walking on water—right into His loving arms.

Then I noticed the high waves crashing around me. First came the information overload and all the treatment decisions. I needed a doctorate degree to understand all the options. Each time I started feeling comfortable with my choice of surgery, drugs, or chemo regimen, I would talk to someone with a different opinion. I'd start second-guessing. Then came the doctors, the media, and well-meaning friends who kept me posted on the latest survival statistics, new studies, new drugs, and new treatments—treatments I didn't receive. Nowadays, it's the news I hear about someone else suffering a recurrence or dying. Sometimes the distractions come from a voice in my own head. It sneaks up on me when I'm praying for someone with cancer, or when my back aches, or when it's time for my annual checkup. *What if I'm not really healed?* Before long, my joy is gone and I'm filled with fear. I'm sinking, right along with Peter.

The same thing can happen to you. Peter sank because he took his eyes off of Jesus and focused on the high waves crashing around him. If we take our eyes off of the Lord's power and focus on our own storms and inadequacies, we pull ourselves out of His presence. When left to our own strength, we can quickly sink into a lake of hopelessness and fear. Peter was afraid, but he had enough sense to cry out for Jesus, his only source of help. Jesus grabbed him, put him back into the boat, and immediately calmed the storm. Peter was safe again, filled with the Lord's peace and the joy of being in His presence.

Often, the true battle to hold on to our joy and fight our fears is in *our minds*. Jesus came to give a life of joy and abundance. Satan's purpose is to steal, kill, and destroy it (John 10:10). Anything that comes into our minds that is contrary to God's Word did not come from Him; it comes from the greatest deceiver of all time. The devil, our great enemy, prowls around like a roaring lion, looking for some victim to devour (1 Peter 5:8–9). And he would like nothing more than for us to take our eyes off of the Lord and step out of His peace and protection so he can pounce on our joy.

But we have nothing to fear. We have Jesus, and He already defeated our enemy on the cross. If we resist him daily with the truth of his defeat, the devil flees (James 4:7). The peace of Christ will come immediately upon us when we bring our fears to God in prayer (Philippians 4:6). He gave us His Holy Spirit and His protective armor so we can stand firm against enemies' attacks (Ephesians 6:13–18). And He gave us His Word. Christ used it as His weapon when Satan tempted Him in the desert, and so can you (Matthew 4:3–10). You can grab your Bible and counter every single lie with a word that refutes it. You can take every lying thought that enters the battlefield of your mind and make it captive to the authority of Jesus (2 Corinthians 10:5). You can keep your peace and joy by staying focused on the truth and keeping Jesus in the center of your life. Remember, in the midst of everything that changes around you, His Word never changes. It stands forever (Isaiah 40:8).

The next time a storm overwhelms you—when you are paralyzed with fear and can't pull yourself out of your deepest despair—cry out to the Lord (Psalm 143:3, 7–8). He knows when your relationship with Him is strong enough to walk on water. And He hears you cry, "Save me, Lord!" when you start to sink into the lake. He's the only one who can really come to your rescue. He might calm the storm, or He might calm your heart.

Either way, you can count on Him to conquer every fear (Psalm 27:1–3). Don't let the enemy use his bag of crafty tricks to steal your joy. Stay so focused on the Lord that nothing distracts you. Let the waves crash, the earthquakes come, and the mountains crumble into the sea. It won't matter. You will not fear because He is there.

Heavenly Father, forgive me when I lose my focus and let the storms of life pull my eyes off of you. Thank you for hearing my cries when I start to sink. I know your perfect love is enough to conquer all my fears. You have already defeated the enemy that threatens to steal my blessing. Help me keep my eyes firmly fixed on you and your Word as the high waves crash around me. Please, Lord, give me the strength to walk in your power. Protect me from the enemy's lies. Protect me from the circumstances that threaten to steal my joy. Calm the storm around me. Calm the storm in my heart. In Jesus' name, amen.

Joy in the Valley

When they walk through the Valley of Weeping,

it will become a place of refreshing springs,

where pools of blessing collect after the rains!

—Psalm 84:6

Four sons could keep a mother very busy. She was relieved when the two oldest boys got their driver's licenses. It sure helped with the trips to town for ball practice, drama, debate, youth and government, and all the other extracurricular activities. The boys were homeschooled and raised in a Christian home. Other than the typical things active boys do, they never gave their parents any trouble. They were just good kids, fun loving, bright, full of life, and a joy to all who knew them.

The accident shocked the entire community. It was a typical night. She made supper for the family, and afterward three of the boys jumped into the car and headed out to their various meetings and practices. The oldest was driving. Suddenly, a car speeding toward them in the oncoming lane swerved out of control and into their lane. The car hit them head on and all three boys were killed instantly. The other driver, a young man in his mid-twenties, was hospitalized for minor injuries, and then arrested and convicted for drunk driving.

In the hours, days, and weeks that followed the accident, she had the opportunity to speak to the media. She gave reason for the hope that strengthened and sustained her. She forgave the young man whose recklessness took the lives of her children. She prayed for him and his parents. Some say the eyes are windows to the soul. If this is true, this mother's soul rested in a very sacred place. I've seen this look in the eyes of others—people suffering cancer or those who have lost something or someone very dear to them. It's a look of supernatural peace that surpasses all human under-standing. It is the outward evidence that Jesus Christ dwells within and stands guard over our hearts and minds (Philippians 4:7). The journey to this sacred place is heartrending and difficult, and few are privileged to go there. We walk through the Valley of Weeping to find it—this sacred place of refreshing springs where pools of blessings collect after the rains (Psalm 84:6). Jesus meets us there. We soon discover He is the only one who can lift us out of the valley.

There are certain things in this life that God can only reveal to us in the midst of a hot, scorching fire. Suffering allows Him to reach into the most hidden places of our souls, where we will feel His presence more clearly than ever before. We may experience His love through other Christians who we never thought would care. Often, those who have experienced our pain become our greatest source of comfort. Jesus himself is no stranger to our suf-fering. He was beaten and flogged with a lead-tipped whip until He was so bloodied and disfigured, no one could tell He was a person (Isaiah 52:14). He was mocked, spat upon, hit on the head with a stick, and forced to wear a crown of long, sharp thorns. He stumbled up the hill to the crucifixion site as He carried a heavy cross on His back. They nailed His hands and feet to the cross and left Him to die a slow, excruciating death (Mark 15:16–37; John 19:17). Through His perfect obedience, Jesus brought us into glory (Hebrews 2:10).

By suffering, Christ shared our human experience and became like us. Remember Him as you weep today. He weeps with you and hears every cry. He feels the sick and empty pit in your stomach. He knows your pain and despair. Now, as you suffer, you grow toward maturity and wholeness to become more like Him (1 Peter 1:15–16). As you become partners with Christ in His suffering, you too are being made holy. And because you share in His suffering, you also share in His victory (1 Peter 4:12–13; 5:10). And the victory is sweet.

Whatever you suffer today, know that the battle will end and your God is already victorious. He can bring good out of the most devastating tragedy (Romans 8:28). A harvest of joy will come from your tears (Psalm 126:5). As you travel with Him down His Highway of Holiness, He will replace your sorrow and mourning with songs of joy and gladness (Isaiah 35:8–10). A double portion of prosperity and everlasting joy will be your inheritance (Isaiah 61:7). Yes, He will restore and strengthen you and place you on a firm foundation (1 Peter 5:10). As the fire burns out, there is a sweet victory you would never taste without God in the center. There is no victory in Christ without sharing in His battle.

Even when all is lost, there is another joy that awaits us—an eternal joy that can never be shaken (Hebrews 10:34). Jesus will return someday to put an end to all our pain (Acts 1:11; Revelation 21:2–4). We live every day with the wonderful expectation of eternal life because of what Christ has done for us on the cross. No matter how much we suffer—no matter how hot the fire—we know it is not our final experience. Christ suffered and died so all who love Him will go to live with Him in a place where death is swallowed up forever and God will wipe away all our tears (Isaiah 25:8). In our deepest despair, we can look at the troubles surrounding us and know they will someday be over. We can look forward to what we have not yet seen—an eternal joy that lasts forever (2 Corinthians 4:18).

Perhaps today you've reached the end of your humanness. You've wandered too long in the Valley of Weeping. If you become bitter over your suffering—if you resent God rather than seek Him—you will never reach the pool of blessing. You will miss out on all the sacred things He wants to show you. You can never force human happiness in the midst of your pain. But you can choose to receive the gift of His supernatural joy in the midst of your deepest sorrow.

Your Father has opened the door of heaven for you. You have an opportunity to step inside and join Him in a place where few will ever go—a sacred place where the Creator of the Universe in all His majesty reaches out and lays His right hand on you. His tender voice says, "Don't be afraid. I am the First and the Last" (Revelation 1:17). An outpouring of peace, love, comfort, and strength flows out of His hand and into your soul. He leads you to a place of refreshing springs, where pools of blessing collect after the rains. You sit at His feet and He reveals remarkable secrets you do not know (Jeremiah 33:3). In the valley of your hopelessness and despair there is an inexplicable joy. The hand of God has lifted you up.

Heavenly Father, my fire is scorching hot. Some days I feel like I can't go on. I've reached the end of my humanness. Thank you for your suffering Son who dwells in me, weeps with me, and never leaves my side. Please, Lord, let me sit with you by the pool of blessing. Lift me up with your mighty hand. Let your peace, comfort, strength, and joy flow through my brokenness. Help me feel the joy of your presence in the depths of my sorrow. Reveal your secrets to me. Let me see your face. In Jesus' name, amen.

MAKE YOUR PEACE
THE FORGIVENESS TEST

If you forgive those who sin against you,

your heavenly Father will forgive you.

—MATTHEW 6:14

NO BITTER ROOT

Watch out that no bitter root of unbelief rises up among you, for whenever it springs up, many are corrupted by its poison.

—HEBREWS 12:15

Cindy was still angry. It had been three years since her husband confessed his indiscretion to her. Eighteen years of marriage and three children. He was a good husband and a wonderful father. How could he do this to her? How long had it been going on? How many times? She was sure there was more to the story, but he insisted she knew everything. He had come to her and tearfully confessed. He apologized and asked for forgiveness. He deeply regretted what he had done. He grieved over it. *Why should she believe him?* He was receiving prayer support from his men's Bible study group, and they were both seeing a Christian counselor.

She knew if their marriage could be saved, it would have to start with forgiveness. She tried so hard to forgive. Sometimes things would feel almost normal again. But then she would see him talking to a woman at church or at a social gathering. Sometimes she wondered about the women he worked with or his customers. She wondered about their friends. She wondered . . . and soon everything would come flooding back. All the hurt and anger would rise up from deep inside and spill out sideways. She would sulk for hours or make a sarcastic remark to remind him of his mistake. Would she ever be able to forgive?

We can all name people in our lives who have hurt us deeply. If we live or work with the offender, we may find ourselves waging an ongoing battle against anger and bitterness. Bitterness can take root deep in our soul and grow like a huge tree that casts a dark shadow over our relationships and blocks the sunshine from our lives. A bitter root can start from hurtful words or unfair treatment by a family member, friend, or co-worker. It might grow from a deep childhood hurt. We continue to feed and water our hurts until our disappointments and unmet expectations grow into resentment, jealousy, and strife.

Time doesn't heal the pain. It only sharpens it. It might lie dormant for a time until a phone call, family gathering, or social event brings it back to life again. Each time we push the rewind button we replay the past hurt in our heads and drive the root of bitterness deeper into our souls. We can carry it around with us for years. But who suffers most? Some say bitterness is like drinking poison and expecting the other person to die! But it never works that way. If we drink the poison—if we choose to take offense—we're the losers.

When Jesus visited His hometown of Nazareth, He couldn't do any mighty miracles there because the people were deeply offended and refused to believe in Him (Mark 6:1–6). Unlike them, if we choose *not* to take offense, God can bless our decision. Jesus healed a Gentile woman's daughter of demon possession simply because she refused to take offense. As she pleaded her case, Jesus tested her by saying, "It isn't right to take food from the children and throw it to the dogs" (Matthew 15:26). Most of us would be deeply offended if someone called us a dog. Instead, she said she would settle for the leftovers, the crumbs from His table. By not taking offense her heart was unblocked. He blessed her instantly and healed her daughter (Matthew 15:27–28).

Taking offense and harboring bitterness against another person will invoke hostility, wound our emotions, and corrupt our spirit.

It violates God's command to love, and it can prevent us from growing in our walk with Christ (Matthew 5:22). Jesus warns us that anger and resentment can hinder our prayers and block our blessing. We can hardly sing our praises and claim to love Him when we feel a deep bitterness toward someone at the same time. Our Lord expects us to go and be reconciled to that person before we come into His presence (Matthew 5:23–24). He tells us to forgive anyone we are holding a grudge against before we come to Him in prayer (Mark 11:25). Deep in her heart, Cindy wanted to be reconciled with her husband and she prayed for her marriage to be restored. She wanted to forgive him, but first, she had to come to terms with her bitterness.

If you feel angry with someone today—if you've allowed bitterness to take root in your soul—you probably understand Cindy's struggle. Sometimes we can get so comfortable with a bitter heart that we just don't want to let go. Bitterness is a poison that corrupts your spirit. Like any poison, it will eventually destroy you. If you allow it to continue growing, you reject God's grace that can set you free. His grace can reach down to the depths of your hurt and bring total healing.

There is no offense committed against you that His perfect love can't cover. Is there a bitter root threatening to corrupt your spirit? Maybe it's time for God to remove it. Ask Him to renew a right spirit within you (Psalm 51:10–13). Ask Him to cleanse you of any resentment or bitterness hidden in your heart (Ephesians 4:31). Ask Him for strength to help you restore your broken relationships (Colossians 3:13). Let Him pluck that bitter root from your soul and replace it with His peace and joy.

Heavenly Father, forgive me for getting comfortable in my bitterness. I'm sorry for nursing my hurts and letting offense and bitterness corrupt my spirit and block my blessing. Lord, thank you that your love and grace covers every offense. Please search me and reveal any bitterness or resentment hidden in the depths of my soul. Cleanse and heal me, and create a right spirit within me. Show me the path of forgiveness and restoration. Fill me with your peace and joy. In Jesus' name, amen.

Leave It to Him

Dear friends, never avenge yourselves. Leave that to God.

For it is written, "I will take vengeance;

I will repay those who deserve it," says the Lord.

—ROMANS 12:19

Beth was at the high point of her career when the hot flames of
testing roared into her life. She worked hard for her academic
degrees and enjoyed a long list of professional achievements before
becoming the high school principal for a major metropolitan
school district. It was a rough first year, and she had to make some
unpopular decisions. A negative attitude pervaded the school. She
was forced to discipline some staff members and correct some
unacceptable practices. A group of teachers began meeting and
complaining to district leadership, but the superintendent assured
Beth of his support. She was stunned when the superintendent
asked for her resignation shortly after she received an excellent
performance review. In the months that followed, Beth replayed
the situation over and over again. What could she have done differently? Colleagues assured her she had acted appropriately. Some
even advised her to file suit against the district for wrongful termi-
nation.

When someone hurts us deeply, we can be very tempted to
take matters into our own hands. It's the way of the world, isn't it?
We live in a day of vengeful lawsuits. Everywhere we turn, people

demand their legal rights. But God's way is different. God wants us to leave it all to Him. We shouldn't pay back evil for evil to anyone (Romans 12:17). He promises to take vengeance on our behalf. Instead of giving those who wrong us what we think they deserve, we should befriend them—give them food if they hunger and water if they thirst. In essence, we should conquer evil with good (Romans 12:20–21). We should respond to the offense with forgiveness (Mathew 5:44).

I know what you must be thinking. *Are you kidding? Do you realize what they did to me?* After much prayer and Christian counsel, Beth discovered the only way to heal from her hurt and escape the fire was to let God have His way. She didn't file suit. She was very careful to speak positively about her superintendent and not malign her former district in her job search. With God's help, she forgave them. She learned that forgiveness can break a cycle of retaliation and lead to a mutual reconciliation. It can make the wrongdoer ashamed of his behavior and lead him to change his ways (Romans 12:20). Even though her supervisor didn't admit to any wrongdoing, he did give an excellent recommendation to Beth's prospective employers. Most important, Beth was free from bitterness and resentment. If any payback was necessary, she left that up to God.

I know. It can be hard to trust God to settle the score, especially when we aren't avenged quickly! God is kind and patient in bringing about His justice (Romans 2:4; 2 Peter 3:9). But He will never leave sin unpunished. We all will eventually have to give an account of our wrongdoings (2 Corinthians 5:10). If we become tired of waiting for God to act and seek revenge on our own, we presume to be smarter than God. We show blatant lack of trust that He will do the right thing. We can trust God's sovereign wisdom to exercise His judgment against those who mistreat us—in His time and His way, not ours.

David understood God's timetable. King Saul was so pleased

with David's musical talent and military successes that he took David into his home and treated him as a son. But his insane jealousy of David soon drove Saul into a murderous rage. David and his loyal followers fled to the hills with Saul and his army in hot pursuit. On two different occasions Saul was an unsuspecting easy target, and David had the opportunity to take revenge. His men begged him to kill Saul and put an end to their plight. Both times, however, David refused (1 Samuel 24:1–7, 26:1–11).

On the first occasion David called out to Saul, "I have not sinned against you even though you have been hunting for me to kill me. . . . Perhaps the Lord will punish you for what you are trying to do to me, but I will never harm you" (1 Samuel 24:11–12). Later on, David says: "May the Lord value my life, even as I have valued yours today. May he rescue me from all my troubles"(1 Samuel 26:24). David left judgment to the Lord. Saul was wounded in battle by the Philistines and died by falling on his own sword (1 Samuel 31). David was anointed king of Judah in his place (2 Samuel 2:4). God avenged David—in His time and His way.

Today, you might be nursing a burning desire to repay those who did you wrong. But when you come face-to-face with injustice, Jesus reminds you not to allow the slightest trace of resentment into your heart (Matthew 5:39–41). The only way you can resist the temptation to handle vengeance on your own is through a personal relationship with Him. When He dwells within you, His *nature* dwells within you. His power will restrain you. His supernatural grace will cover you.

Jesus knows you've been wronged, misunderstood, hurt, and maligned. He's been there. He suffered at the hands of the public, the religious community, and the government. Through it all He remained silent. He left vindication to His Father and loved His persecutors (Luke 23:34). And with His power, so can you. His promises are great for those who show kindness to their enemies

(Luke 6:35). You can trust Him to do the right thing. The next time you're tempted to avenge yourself, leave it to Him.

Heavenly Father, forgive me for taking matters into my own hands against those who have hurt me. I'm sorry for my thoughts of revenge and any actions I have taken against them. Forgive me for not trusting you to administer justice on my behalf. Thank you for your wisdom and for the Holy Spirit that gives me the power to remain silent in the face of persecution. If justice is in order, I trust you to avenge me in your time and in your way. Please help me show your love and kindness to my enemies. In Jesus' name, amen.

Choose to Pray

Pray for the happiness of those who curse you.

Pray for those who hurt you.

—Luke 6:28

It was morning rush hour on a cold mid-January Tuesday. Howie's car slowed to a standstill. It was still dark outside. A string of headlights and taillights stretched out in front of him as far as he could see. He didn't mind the traffic. It gave him time to think about the day ahead and make his mental "to do" list. This morning, his mind was busy mapping out sales targets. He was optimistic. It was a New Year and a new start. Business took a hit after 9/11, but he was confident that the new customers and promising new markets he had worked so hard to win would continue to make up for the loss. He would sit down with each of his direct reports over the next few weeks and discuss sales goals for their territories. He felt good about his team. There were problems in the past, but with some personnel changes and good coaching, he had pulled them through the rough spots. After several trips overseas, he was convinced senior management understood the challenges his division faced and his strategies for overcoming the changing market conditions.

The sun was up as he pulled into his parking space and made his way to the office. He would try to set up some time with his boss this morning to go over his projections. The boss beat him to it. He asked Howie to meet him after lunch. Good. Enough time to put some forecasts in writing, in between all the phone calls and meetings that typically filled his schedule.

As usual, the morning passed quickly. He worked through lunch, gathered up some notes, and headed for the boss's office. He settled into the chair on the other side of the massive desk. His boss got up and closed the door. A long silence passed between them. "We're letting you go." The words hung in the air. Howie couldn't believe he had heard correctly. "You're kidding." His boss repeated, "We're letting you go."

Still in a daze, Howie walked back to his office and started packing. His co-workers watched as he carried boxes of personal items out to the car. They watched, and no one said a word. No one said good-bye when he headed out the door for the last time. He got into the car and headed back to the freeway. The traffic was moving slowly. Time to think; time to process what had just happened. Time to pray.

Some would call him crazy, but yes, he prayed. He prayed for his boss. He prayed for the managers overseas who had made the decision to replace him. He prayed for his sales team, his co-workers, and his customers. He prayed for the company to prosper. He prayed because God commanded him to pray. God commanded him to love his enemies and pray for those who persecute him. He knew it wasn't enough for a true child of God to love only those who loved him. No, even non-believers are kind to their friends. He knew his Father in heaven expected much more from him (Matthew 5:43–48; Luke 6:32–33).

Howie isn't perfect. He's aspiring to achieve Christ-like character and holy living just like the rest of us. But he's discovered something about Christian love in the process. We all find it very difficult to *feel* love and forgiveness toward the people who hurt us. And it's totally against our human sensibilities to actually *pray* for them. When Jesus told us to love our enemies, He wasn't talking about our feelings. He was talking about our actions. He was talking about our will.

Christian love is not a feeling. God doesn't expect us to *feel* love for anyone who hurts us deeply. Instead, we can choose to *show* love and kindness through our actions purely out of obedience to Him. And His instructions are very clear: "If someone slaps you on one cheek, turn the other cheek. If someone demands your coat, offer your shirt also. Give what you have to anyone who asks you for it; and when things are taken away from you, don't try to get them back. Do for others as you would like them to do for you"(Luke 29:29–31). Instead of striking back at his former employers, Howie chose to treat them with kindness and respect. He cooperated when they needed information and expected nothing in return. He encouraged his own loyal sales reps and customers to stay with the company. He didn't get angry. He didn't sue. When they hurt him deeply, he chose to respond with love.

Can you? In your fire today, remember that the person who hurt you—the boss who fired you, the spouse who left you, the friend who betrayed you, or the family member who rejected you—bears the image of God (Genesis 1:26). Regardless of their crime against you, God loves them (Romans 5:8). He sends sunlight and rain on both evil and good people (Matthew 5:45). And He commands you to love them in the same way He loves you (John 15:12).

But He also knows you can't love your enemies on your own power. As you suffer with Jesus, He'll start replacing your heart with His. He'll give you the strength to love like He loved. And He loved the whole world even though it rebelled against Him. An amazing thing happens when you choose to act in love. God uses you as a vessel to express *His* love. His character is reflected in you. The world sees that Jesus is Lord of your life. So ask the Holy Spirit to help you take action. With His help, overcome evil with good (Romans 12:21). Give your enemies the same respect you desire for yourself. Give as though you are giving to God. Tell that person who hurt you so deeply that you want to reconcile. Send a card or a gift. Smile a little. Show some kindness. Choose to pray. With His help, your feelings might catch up.

Heavenly Father, sometimes it feels like you expect too much of me! But then I remember that you never leave me to my own humanness. Forgive me for not showing kindness and respect to those who have sinned against me. I know I can never love them or pray for them on my own strength. Thank you for your Son, who died for the sins of the entire world in one act of perfect love. Lord, please give me the strength to choose love. Give me opportunities to show kindness to my enemies. Show me how to turn the other cheek and to treat others the way I want to be treated. Show me how to pray for those who have deeply hurt me. In Jesus' name, amen.

Forgive Like Jesus

But if you refuse to forgive others,
your Father will not forgive your sins.

—Matthew 6:15

Andy was a bright young man living his dream job as activities director for a major metropolitan school district. He was devoted to his family and the community, and he made some innovative changes in the district. He also made some mistakes. He said some things he shouldn't have said. Some jokes and comments he made after work hours were taken out of context and repeated to others. He was completely stunned when some staff members filed a complaint of sexual harassment. The district conducted a cursory investigation and gave him a choice to resign or be terminated.

Instead, he chose to fight in arbitration. He believed in his innocence and was confident that the truth would prevail. During the hearing, he was devastated when several witnesses he thought were friends lied and misquoted him. Others who planned to speak on his behalf were afraid of losing their jobs if they testified. Several facts were hidden from his lawyers so they were unable to adequately prepare his defense. In the end, he lost. The district terminated him. A further investigation into his licensure found him not guilty, but by then, the damage was done.

Throughout his ordeal, a community of Christians surrounded Andy and his family with support and prayer. People brought food, took care of his children, and helped him look for work. God supplied all his needs. When no other school district would hire him, he found a good job outside his profession and moved to a new community to start over. His house sold just in time for exactly the right price. As the hot fire slowly turns to ashes, Andy is learning that the world isn't always fair, but God is always faithful. Andy and his wife found God in the fire and it changed their lives. They will never be the same.

He wondered if he could ever forgive those who lied about him. Why *should* he? These people nearly ruined his life! The reason he should forgive is evident every time we say the Lord's Prayer. In it, we ask God to forgive us our sins *just as we forgive those who have sinned against us* (Luke 11:4). Think about it. Jesus took the sinful nature of the entire human race upon His back. He forgave us for rebelling against Him and opened the door for reconciliation with the Father while we still rejected Him (Romans 5:8). Beaten and bloodied, He looked down into the faces of those who mocked and tortured Him and cried, "Father, forgive these people, because they don't know what they are doing" (Luke 23:34).

Jesus set the benchmark for forgiveness on the cross. He forgave us, so He expects us to forgive others (Colossians 3:13). He *chose* to forgive. Can we ever forgive others to the same degree that God forgives us? We can, but only when we begin to understand what Christ did for us and how much He loves us, when we personally experience His grace. Only then can we begin to forgive those who sin against us, and only by His power and might.

Perhaps you've tried to forgive but you simply can't. Or maybe you've made a conscious choice not to forgive your enemies. By forgiving those who have hurt us, we are not excusing their misdeeds. We're forgiving them in spite of their sin—just as Christ did for us. If we choose forgiveness and treat our enemies with grace and compassion, these qualities will come back to us in full mea-

sure (Luke 6:38). But when we harbor deep anger and unforgive-
ness toward those who hurt us, it can block our blessing and
hinder our relationship with God. We can't claim to love God and
lift our voices in praise while holding on to a grudge at the same
time. Jesus said we can pray for anything, and if we believe, we
will have it. But we need to *first* forgive and be reconciled with
our enemies so our Father in heaven can forgive us (Mark 11:24–
25).

Today, you might feel a lot like Andy. Maybe you're nursing
some very deep wounds at the hands of your enemy. Andy has a
family who loves him and Christian mentors who support him and
pray with him. He repented of his mistakes. He's praying for help
to move forward with his life. He's praying for a deeper relationship with the Lord and a greater understanding of His ways. He's
praying for God to help him forgive. And so can you.

Do you really want God to forgive you *in the same way* you are
forgiving those who hurt you? Forgiveness is a choice. It's not a
skill, a spiritual gift, or a special character trait. It's not something
you can do on your own power. If you try, guilt and shame will
likely follow. You will never meet God's measure of forgiveness on
your own power; ask Him today for the supernatural strength to
forgive others like He forgives you. Then the next time you say
the Lord's Prayer and ask Him to forgive your sins as you forgive
those who sin against you, you can say it with your heart. A forgiving spirit demonstrates you have truly received the Spirit of
God. When the power of the Holy Spirit dwells within you, forgiveness can become as natural as breathing. You can forgive like
Jesus.

*Heavenly Father, forgive me for claiming to love you while I hold
grudges against those who have hurt me. Thank you for taking the sins
of the world upon yourself. Lord, you set the benchmark for forgiveness
when you died for me. Thank you that your grace covers me even as I*

struggle to show grace to others. I want to be able to forgive those who sin against me, just as you forgave those who persecuted you. I know I can only forgive through the power of the Holy Spirit that dwells within me. Lord, give me a deeper understanding of you and your ways. Help me forgive like you. In Jesus' name, amen.

LET PEACE RULE

And let the peace that comes from Christ rule in your hearts. For as members of one body you are all called to live in peace.

—COLOSSIANS 3:15

Jill was a go-getter—a no-nonsense, get-it-done type of person. And she had more experience than most of her co-workers. When she was hired, her supervisor thought the department could benefit from Jill's background and strong faith. She had met Jill through a job search group at her church. Jill wasted no time. She streamlined processes. She revised outdated marketing materials. She reached out to previous customers and won back their business. When something needed to be done, Jill did it. If a problem needed solving, she solved it. She didn't see a need to bother the rest of the team. She liked the job.

But lately, it was becoming more and more difficult to go to work. Her heart began pounding as soon as she walked in the door. People huddled up in hushed conversation would suddenly stop talking when she walked into the office. Conversation with her was curt and focused only on work. No one invited her to lunch anymore. Her supervisor was pleased at first, but lately, she was giving Jill the cold shoulder along with the rest of the team. Jill was miserable. She had taken the job because it was a Christian company. She didn't understand what she had done wrong. What should she do?

Jesus was very clear about what we should do when another believer sins against us. Often, our first impulse is to withdraw in resentment, seek revenge, or engage in gossip. But Jesus instructed us to go *first* to that person in love and bring the sin to their attention. When we choose to speak the truth in love, our goal is to restore the offender's relationship with God and fellow Christians so we can live in harmony. We always need to check our own heart before appointing ourselves the official "truth teller." Our purpose should not be to point out every sin or attack of every person who hurts us or does us wrong! We need to ask ourselves: Do we truly love the offender with Christian love, and are we willing to forgive? We'll never help the person who sinned against us unless our rebuke is tied to forgiveness (Matthew 18:15–17).

Jill's first reaction was to quit her job. If it weren't for a friend from her church who worked in another department, she would have. She was hurt and angry over the way she was treated. But her friend prayed with her and encouraged her to go talk to her supervisor. Jill set up the meeting and prayed for God to supply the right words. When they met, she had the opportunity to share several incidents that hurt her. She explained how the office climate made her feel. Her supervisor apologized for not supporting Jill's role in the office with her co-workers. She apologized for not being honest and forthright about correcting some performance and work style issues. Jill's supervisor asked for forgiveness, and Jill forgave her. Then her supervisor called a meeting with the entire team. People shared their feelings and exchanged apologies. Communication channels opened and the team began to heal.

It's never easy to confront the tough issues. It's much easier to gossip, complain, and nurse our wounds than to seek reconciliation. Jesus used one of His many parables to illustrate how serious He was about forgiveness. He compared His kingdom to a king who decided to bring his accounts up to date. One of his servants owed him millions of dollars he couldn't pay, so the king ordered him to sell everything he owned to pay the debt. But when the servant begged for forgiveness, the king was filled with pity and forgave his debt. Then this same man, who had been forgiven, went to a fellow servant who owed him a few thousand dollars and demanded instant payment. When the second servant begged for a little more time, his creditor had him arrested and jailed. Soon word got back to the king. "Shouldn't you have mercy on your fellow servant, just as I had mercy on you?" he demanded. The king sent the man to prison until he had paid every penny. And then Jesus said: "That's what my heavenly Father will do to you if you refuse to forgive your brothers and sisters in your heart" (Matthew 18:33, 35).

These are tough words to hear from the King of Kings who forgave our debt and paid for the sins of the world. Yes, Jesus expects us to forgive our Christian brothers and sisters who sin against us. He gives us clear instructions for how to resolve conflict and reconcile with them. And He gives us clear instructions for living in peace with one another. He said we must make allowances for each other's faults (Colossians 3:13). Perhaps you're living or working in close quarters with another believer who has offended you. It could be a spouse, a child, a parent, or a co-worker. How many times do you have to forgive? Jesus said we shouldn't bother to keep track. We should forgive someone who is truly repentant no matter how many times they ask—seventy times seven if necessary (Matthew 18:21–22; Luke 17:4).

After experiencing God's gracious favor and His gift of redemption on the cross, how can we possibly withhold forgiveness from others? When we choose not to forgive, we lift ourselves above God's law of love. And His law of love is very clear. As God's children, we must clothe ourselves with mercy, kindness, humility, gentleness, and patience. But the most important piece of clothing we will ever wear is *love*. As members of one body, the love of Christ binds us all together in perfect harmony (Colossians

3:12–14). When you choose love and forgiveness, all your differences, arguments, and hurts become irrelevant. With God's power, you can live and work together in peace instead of cold silence or open conflict. Start now. Reconcile your Christian relationships with a healthy dose of Jesus. Let peace rule.

Heavenly Father, forgive me for gossiping, harboring resentment, and turning my back on fellow believers when they sin against me. Forgive me for not speaking truth and withholding my forgiveness. Thank you for your gift of redemption and the love that binds us together in perfect harmony. Please give me strength and boldness to go to the person who offended me and speak the truth in love. Help me make allowances for the faults of my Christian brothers and sisters. Let me be an instrument of reconciliation. Let the peace of Christ rule in my heart. In Jesus' name, amen.

ALWAYS BE THANKFUL
THE GRATITUDE TEST

No matter what happens, always be thankful, for this is God's will

for you who belong to Christ Jesus.

—1 THESSALONIANS 5:18

Praise God First!

The king appointed singers to walk ahead of the army,

singing to the LORD and praising him for his holy splendor.

This is what they sang: "Give thanks to the LORD;

his faithful love endures forever!"

—2 Chronicles 20:21

Naturally, King Jehoshaphat was alarmed when he heard that a vast army of Moabites, Ammonites, and Menuites were mounting an attack against him. He called for a fast and gathered all the people of Judah and Jerusalem together for prayer in front of the Lord's temple. As he prayed, God sent word that the people should not be afraid or discouraged, for the battle was not theirs to fight. He told them to take their positions, stand still, and watch the Lord's victory. He promised He would be with them, and they would not even need to fight! At these words, the king and all the people bowed down, worshiped, and lifted up shouts of praise to the Lord (2 Chronicles 20:1–19).

Early the next morning, on the way into battle, the king stopped to encourage the people: "Believe in the Lord your God, and you will be able to stand firm" (2 Chronicles 20:20). And then he did the strangest thing. Instead of sending the men in to fight, he appointed singers to walk ahead of the army and give praise to the Lord. Imagine what the enemy was thinking. They expected a fierce army, but instead faced a praise chorus singing, "Give thanks to the Lord; his faithful love endures forever!" (2 Chronicles 20:21). At the sound of their voices, the Lord set the enemy armies into confusion, and they fought against one another. When the army of Judah arrived at the lookout point in the wilderness, enemy soldiers lay dead on the ground as far as they could see. Not a single one escaped, and not a single Israelite was killed. There was so much equipment, clothing, and other valuables that it took the people three days to collect all the plunder. Finally, on the fourth day, they gathered at this place they named the Valley of Blessing to praise and thank the Lord for their victory.

It took courage and a lot of faith for King Jehoshaphat to march into battle with a band of praise singers leading the charge, instead of a band of warriors. When the enemy has us pinned against the wall, our first instinct is to fight back. But in times of deep distress, our first step should be to get into a right relationship with God. Jesus taught us to praise God *first,* and then lift our requests up to Him in prayer (Luke 11:1–4). We open our lines of communication with Him through praise and thanksgiving. Even in the deepest despair, we can find cause for thankfulness. Once the communication channel is open, His ears are open to our cries for help. Our praises have released His power; now He can do His part. He can calm our fears, lift our distress, supply our needs, and show us His goodness. Now He can rescue us from the fire (Psalm 34:1–8).

That's exactly what Ellen did. News traveled fast when doctors confirmed her cancer had returned. She was a devoted volunteer at church, and her hands touched just about everything. Everyone knew Ellen. The bad news came on Wednesday, a church meeting night. It felt like a mighty army marching against her, an army she thought had been defeated. Singing praises to the Lord was not her first impulse! Beating cancer with every medical weapon in the arsenal seemed like a much better battle plan, but even the best treatment offered no guarantee of victory.

Ellen didn't have an army of musicians to send ahead. But there she stood, in the front of the church at Wednesday night service, arms raised to the heavens, singing praises to her King. After worship, she went into the prayer chapel with her family for healing prayer. Ellen opened up communication with the Father through praise and thankfulness. When she cried out to Him in prayer, she gave Him control of the cancer. She made it His battle, not hers, and God heard her cries for help. He reached down His mighty hand and lifted her out of the fire.

Are you looking for victory today? Maybe you're tired of fighting the flames on your own. You're ready for God to reach in and pull you out of the furnace. Probably praise and thanksgiving are the furthest things from your mind. But maybe it's time to unleash the power. . . . Open your Bible and meditate on psalms of praise. Listen to praise music. Go find a Spirit-filled worship service. Raise your hands up to the heavens and shout praises to your King! Thank Him for His unfailing love and His tender mercies. Thank Him for the blessings He has poured on you and your family. Thank Him for the fellowship you have with other believers. Thank Him for the assurance of eternity. Thank Him for fighting your battle today. Your enemy may have formed an army against you, but His Son already defeated it for you at the cross. And you don't have to wait for Him to deliver the victory to start celebrating. He hears your praises and He hears your cries for help. Soon that fiery furnace—that deep valley of suffering—will become your Valley of Blessing. Praise God first—His faithful love endures forever!

Heavenly Father, I'm sorry for focusing on my battle instead of praising you. You are an awesome and merciful God! I give thanks to you, Lord, for you are good! I sing your praises and lift your name on high. You are exalted in the heavens and over all the earth. You are my

King and your faithful love endures forever! Thank you, Lord, for all you have done for me. You fill my life with good things. You forgive my sins and redeem my life from destruction. Lord, please hear my cry! I'm tired of fighting on my own. My battle belongs to you. Set me free from my fears. Lift my distress and come to my rescue! In Jesus' name, amen.

BREAD FROM HEAVEN

"Why have you brought us out of Egypt to die here in the wilderness?" they complained. "There is nothing to eat here and nothing to drink. And we hate this wretched manna!"

—NUMBERS 21:5

If you've ever cooked for fussy eaters, then you know how Moses felt. Every morning in the wilderness, on the way to the Promised Land, the Israelites woke up to a miracle. Manna—bread from heaven—covered the ground like thin flakes of frost. It was white like coriander seed, and it tasted like honey cakes (Exodus 16:31). It was a gift from God that came every day in just the right amount. The people gathered it and ground it into flour like grain. But soon, it wasn't enough. "Give us meat!" they complained to Moses. "We hate this wretched manna!"

The Israelites didn't seem to notice what God was doing for them anymore. They forgot how He had delivered them from a brutal life of slavery in Egypt and had provided for their every need. He was making them into a chosen nation and giving them a new land, and all they could think about was the delicious food they left behind. "There is nothing to eat here!" they whined to Moses. "Why have you brought us out of Egypt to die in the wilderness? Oh, for some meat!" (Numbers 11:4–6, 21:5).

Dissatisfaction and complaining arise when we stop being grateful for what we *do* have and start focusing on what we *don't* have. The Israelites thought it was their right to have more. Their complaining came from several sources. They refused to obey God's laws (Psalm 78:10). They also doubted God's ability to care for them, in spite of the spectacular miracles He had done before them (Psalm 78:11–12, 19–20). They were stubborn, rebellious, and unfaithful people who refused to give their hearts to God (Psalm 78:8). They complained about their unmet needs to each other and to their leaders, instead of praying to God.

They finally got their meat—so much that the Lord promised they would eat it until they gagged! He sent so much quail that each person gathered no less than fifty bushels. However, they also paid dearly for rejecting the Lord's help and approaching Him with a sinful covetous attitude. The Lord struck the camp with a severe plague while they were still eating the meat, the meat they had desired more than God (Numbers 11:20; 31–35).

I don't know about you, but it's easy for me to stand back and think, *Oh, what a wretched people they were!* But before we judge the Israelites, perhaps we need to take a look at ourselves. We can be just as stubborn, rebellious, and disobedient. How often do we whine to our friends and family members before we take our desires and needs to God? It's especially tempting to complain in the heat of fire. *After all we're going through, don't we have the right to complain?*

When I was going through chemotherapy, there was a lot I could complain about. First of all, I had *cancer*. This was no small thing. I could complain that I was bald and lived for months without hair, eyebrows, or eyelashes. I could complain about weekly trips to the hospital, IV needles, nausea, and an uncertain future. Or I could focus on the good things God was doing in my life, like the miracle that discovered the cancer in the first place, or the skillful surgeon who removed the tumor and preserved my breast. I could focus on the leading oncologist who provided the most cutting-edge treatment available to me, and most important, the prayers and support of a loving family and thoughtful friends.

We can be so preoccupied with what God isn't doing for us and so focused on getting what we think we deserve that we quickly forget about God's mercies. We can fall into the swirl of whining and complaining and forget about all the good things He does for us. When I forget, King David gives me a list of reminders:

- He forgives all our sins and heals our diseases.
- He ransoms us from death and surrounds us with love and tender mercies.
- He fills our lives with good things and renews our youth like the eagle's.
- He gives righteousness and justice for us when we are treated unfairly (Psalm 103:3–6).

In the midst of our ungratefulness, we can take comfort in knowing our Father's steadfast love and tender mercy is greater than any sin. His mercies start fresh every day to keep us from complete destruction. His unfailing love never ends (Lamentations 3:22–24). He pours His blessings on us, even if we don't deserve a single one. He provided for the Israelites in the wilderness and promises to provide for you and me (Philippians 4:19). And He promises even more. Just as our earthly supply is temporal and physical, the manna sustained the Israelites only for a day. But in His mercy, God gave us Jesus, the true bread from heaven. He satisfies us completely and gives us eternal life (John 6:58).

Are you grateful for the manna, or are you crying for some meat? The next time the fire burns hot and you're tempted to complain, take a look at David's list. Read it every day until it becomes permanently etched on your heart. Never forget God's gifts of life, health, family, food, shelter, work, and friends. Never forget His faithfulness. If you can approach every day with a grateful heart, you can take all your requests to the Lord in prayer, and a complaining spirit will never take hold in your soul. You'll always remember that the good things in your life—all things good and perfect—come directly from your Father in heaven (James 1:17). He can supply all your needs from His glorious riches (Philippians 4:19). All His blessings and tender mercies are yours in Jesus, your true Bread from heaven.

Heavenly Father, forgive me for complaining to others about my unmet needs and for being ungrateful in the midst of my suffering. I'm sorry for doubting your desire and ability to care for me. Thank you for your tender mercies that start fresh every day! Thank you for all my blessings. Great is your faithfulness! I know you can supply all my needs from your heavenly storehouse. Please give me a grateful heart. Help me focus on all the good things you are doing in my life, even the things I don't yet understand. In Jesus' name, amen.

LET YOUR LIFE OVERFLOW

Let your lives overflow with thanksgiving for all he has done.

—COLOSSIANS 2:7

She stood in front of the mirror, amazed at her thick black hair and her body restored to health. The sounds of family and friends laughing in the background as they gathered to celebrate her daughter's graduation brought a smile to her face. A few years earlier, she sat bald and broken at the Lord's feet. Chemotherapy may have stolen her hair and her dignity, but the cancer threatened to steal her dreams. In that bald dark place filled with doctor visits, needles, test results, and uncertainty, she came face-to-face with Jesus, and in His mercy, He healed her!

She drops to her knees to praise and thank her God and King. Death had its hands around her throat, and she could only see a future of trouble and sorrow. But she called on the Lord to save her, and He bent down and snatched her from the fire. She lifts her arms up to the heavens and praises Him with songs of joy. She gives thanks to the Lord, for He is good (Psalm 63:4–5, 116:2–4, 136:1). The reality of His grace and mercy touches the deepest caverns of her soul. Her life overflows with thanksgiving.

The young man stands at the front of the church waiting for his beautiful bride to appear. A joyful anticipation fills the room as he looks into the faces of family and friends who loved, supported, and prayed for him. A few years earlier, he sat broken at the Lord's feet. He was one of the troubled teens he now so faithfully serves in his ministry—a chemically dependent high school dropout on the road to self-destruction. He lied, stole, and partied his way from one jail cell to the next. After several failed attempts at court-ordered rehab, a judge sent him to a Christian residential treatment program for substance abuse.

In this dark place of despair and hopelessness, he met Jesus face-to-face. He cried out for the Lord to save him from complete destruction. He asked Him to wash away his sin, remove the stain of his guilt, and create a pure heart and spirit within him (Psalm 51:7–10). The Lord heard his cry and lifted him out of the fiery pit of addiction. He set his feet on solid ground and steadied him as he walked along a new path of freedom—a chemical-free life-style, a college degree, a good job, and a beautiful Christian woman to marry. The Lord gave him a new song to sing (Psalm 40:1–3). As she walks down the aisle toward him, he vows to sing praises to his King as long as he lives, even with his dying breath (Psalm 146:2)! He drinks deeply from the well of God's grace and mercy. His life overflows with thanksgiving.

Over two thousand years ago, there was another man whose life overflowed with gratitude. Just outside a border village between Galilee and Samaria, ten lepers cried out to Jesus for healing. In those days, leprosy was a highly contagious condition, so those who suffered from it were social outcasts. They were forbidden from entering their villages, living in their own homes, or touching their loved ones. Jesus sent all ten lepers to the priest to be declared clean as required by the law of Moses. On the way to the priest, their leprosy disappeared! They responded in faith to Jesus' command, and He healed them. But only one leper returned to *thank* Him. The other nine went off to celebrate the good news of their healing with family and friends. Only a Samaritan—a member of a race despised by the Jews—considered the source of his blessing. He fell face down on the ground at the feet of Jesus to thank and worship Him for giving him back his life (Luke 17:11–19).

Only when we come to terms with our brokenness and our desperate need for a Savior can we truly appreciate the scope of God's grace and mercy. Our response to this knowledge is overwhelming gratitude. The Samaritan understood, and so did the sinful woman—a prostitute—who knelt and wept at Jesus' feet. As her tears fell on His feet, she wiped them off with her hair and anointed His feet with expensive perfume. Sensing His host's indignation, Jesus taught that forgiveness is for *all* His followers, regardless of the gravity of their sin. He contrasted the woman's heartfelt generosity with His host's stingy hospitality. In this lavish act of love, she showed that the measure of our gratefulness corresponds to the measure of the Lord's forgiveness. Jesus said, "I tell you, her sins—and they are many—have been forgiven, so she has shown me much love. But a person who is forgiven little shows only little love" (Luke 7:47).

Yes, God honors a grateful heart. Everything in our lives—our work, our play, our worship, and our prayers—should be saturated with thanksgiving to God (Philippians 4:6–7). When He hears your cries of despair—when He snatches you from the fire and saves your life from destruction—how do you respond? Do you rush off to celebrate like the nine lepers? Or do you look beyond your answered prayers to the source of your blessings? Fall to your knees and give thanks to the Lord! Let your tears of gratitude spill on His feet as you give glory to His name. Think of it! Your sins may be many and your need may be great, but you have been restored and forgiven by the Son of God! You are free to walk in the abundant life He so graciously won for you. As you step into your glorious future, never forget what the Lord has done. Lift your hands to the heavens and sing praises to your King. Let your life overflow with thanksgiving!

Heavenly Father, forgive my ungratefulness. Purify me from my sin. Wash me so I will be whiter than snow! Create in me a clean heart and renew a right spirit within me. Oh Lord, I'm alone and broken! Please bend down and snatch me from the fire. Save my life from destruction. I fall to my knees and thank you for your grace, your mercy, and your unfailing love. I lift my arms to the heavens and sing praises to your name! Thank you for lifting me out of the pit of despair and setting my feet on solid ground. Guide and protect me as I walk along a new path of freedom in your Son. My life overflows with thanksgiving! In Jesus' name, amen.

YOUR ROYAL HERITAGE

And now that you belong to Christ,

you are the true children of Abraham. You are his heirs,

and now all the promises God gave to him belong to you.

—GALATIANS 3:29

When we walk closely with the Lord, He loves to bless us. He knows our deepest desires and dreams. Lisa dreamed of opening a little Christian bookshop and café—a cozy place where friends could gather to browse the latest Christian titles, study the Bible together, shop for inspirational gifts, and share a cup of latte. She prayed, planned, and saved for years to see her dream come true.

When her husband moved the family to a new community, the dream came within her grasp. They could afford to lease space, and her shop was a perfect fit for the artistic town where vacationers perused the quaint little boutiques lining the streets. Her plans were falling into place when her husband made an unexpected announcement: He was leaving her. The divorce settlement shattered her dreams—both the promise of raising a family together with the man she loved and her vision for the little bookshop.

As grief overwhelmed her, something inside Lisa wouldn't let the dream die. She prayed desperately for God to show her a way to support herself and her children. Hope flickered when a perfect building went up for sale in the heart of town. But it quickly died again when she learned the down payment was out of her reach.

In the heat of the fire, Lisa found strength in the Lord. She read her Bible and prayed every day. The days turned into weeks, until one day a call came from a Realtor who had heard of her interest in the building. The down payment had been lowered—it was exactly the figure she could afford. Exactly. No one knew how much she had to spend. No one knew but God.

From that point on she was blessed by the unexpected—a dear friend who needed a place to live would work in the shop for room and board; vendors offered surprisingly generous terms; people donated store fixtures and furniture; a creative and experienced Christian retailer wandered into the shop while on vacation and spent three days helping her unpack and display merchandise for the grand opening. God knew Lisa's heart. She was grateful for His loving-kindness and faithfulness in her life. He was delighted to bless His precious daughter who continued to be obedient to Him even in the midst of great difficulty.

When we accept Christ as our Savior, we too become children of the Almighty God (Galatians 3:26). As soon as He adopts us into His family, He sends His Spirit to dwell in our hearts and gives us permission to call Him Father (Galatians 4:6). And our Father delights in showering us with blessings at times and in ways we don't expect. If you're a parent, this should come as no surprise. We know exactly what our child wants—we've known for months. We shop until we find the perfect gift. We wrap it carefully and find the perfect hiding place until that special day arrives. Then we look forward with excitement to that moment when our child will tear off the wrapping paper and open the box. What a joy to watch the look of delight on his or her face! In the same way, God takes great joy in our delight when He opens up the heavenly storehouse and showers us with unexpected gifts.

There's no lack of supply in His heavenly storehouse. In fact, as children of God, everything He has belongs to us (Galatians 4:7). Do you realize what that means? As true children of Abraham, we are entitled to the same spiritual blessings God promised him (Galatians 3:29). If we obey the Lord and walk in His ways, He will bless us wherever we go and in whatever we do. He will conquer our enemies when they attack and scatter them in seven directions! We have direct access to our Creator and Father, and He has claimed us as His very own. He promises to care for our every need at the proper time from His rich heavenly treasury. The entire world will stand in awe of the blessings God pours on His children (Deuteronomy 28:1–13)!

Now, that's reason for gratitude. Lisa learned there is plenty in God's heavenly treasury. His glorious riches were more than enough to supply her every need (Philippians 4:19). And do you know what? If Christ is your Lord and Savior—if you have a heart that seeks to obey Him and walk in His ways—your royal heritage entitles you to the very same promises.

The same Father who took care of Lisa will take care of you. He knows exactly what you need. He knows every dream and every desire. He's carefully preparing each blessing until the timing is perfect. He's looking forward to the look of delight on your face when He blesses you with a long-awaited answer to a desperate prayer, unexpected help in a time of need, or an encouraging word in the midst of the fire. So go boldly into the throne room and thank your Father for your blessings (Hebrews 4:16). He loves to shower you with gifts from His heavenly treasury. After all, you're a member of the royal family; you're the child of a King.

Heavenly Father, I know there is plenty in your royal treasury to meet all my needs. Forgive me when I doubt your supply or your desire to bless me. I'm sorry for taking your gifts for granted. Lord, you know my dreams and the desires of my heart. Thank you for my royal heritage and the abundance of good things you pour into my life. Thank you for the unexpected blessings. Lord, help me to obey you and walk in your ways. In Jesus' name, amen.

THE INDESCRIBABLE GIFT

Thank God for his Son—a gift too wonderful for words!

—2 CORINTHIANS 9:15

What did she have to be thankful for? Only a few short months ago, the war on terror hit home. Her beautiful son, Corey, a career military officer, was shot down while piloting a secret rescue mission over the mountains of Afghanistan. In the weeks and months that follow, she grieves. She cries out to God from the most secret places of her soul. She comes face-to-face with her own helplessness and how desperately she needs a Savior—a personal Redeemer who knows her every thought, emotion, and fear, a Savior who feels her pain and cries her tears. She finds comfort in His presence. She treasures her daily quiet times. She prays, reflects on her life, and finds comfort in His Word. The more she seeks Him, the more she finds Him. His grace and tender mercies carry her through the pain of living each day without her son.

Something amazing happens. At the core of her grief, her heart floods with gratefulness—not bitterness and despair over all she has lost, but deep gratitude to God for all she has gained, blessing upon blessing! She sees His sovereign hand in every detail—from the friends and family who love her and the husband who adores her to the birth of her beautiful children and the gift of her precious grandchildren. She reflects daily on the gift of her son and how his life continues to bless so many people. She gives thanks for each childhood memory and for the privilege of being his mother. She gives thanks for the gift of eternal life and the coming day when she will stroll with him down heavenly streets of gold. She gives thanks for the promise that *all* things work together for the good of those who love Him (Romans 8:28). She knows He will use her sorrow for His glory. She admits it isn't easy. Grief is an emotional roller coaster, and the pain comes flooding back without any warning. But she has reason for hope. She received an indescribable gift in the heat of the fire—she met Jesus face-to-face. She clings to Him tightly and won't let go.

It isn't easy when all is lost, the fire roars, and the pain is so intense we can barely make it through the day. But there is reason for hope. There is reason to be grateful. Of all God's blessings, there is one greater than all the others—the gift of His Son. Before God gave us this perfect gift, we were held captive to a law we could never follow. He knew all along we were prisoners to our sin with no hope of escape, and in His mercy He orchestrated the perfect escape plan. He sent His Son to set us free. On the cross at Calvary, Jesus shed His blood and died. He paid the debt for our sin. Only those who place their faith in Him are made right in God's sight and set free from sin's grasp.

It doesn't matter who we are or what we have done. It is only by God's grace that we are saved. Whoever receives His Son receives the free gift of eternal life (Romans 3:20–25; Ephesians 2:8–10; John 3:16). Our salvation is an awesome promise of things to come. No matter how deep our sorrow or how hot the fire, we can take comfort in knowing that our entire life on this earth is just a moment to God. Human existence is but a breath to Him (Psalm 39:5). But the precious gift of His Son promises an *eternal* home where sorrow and mourning will disappear—a place where all the faithful will be reunited and sing songs of everlasting joy and gladness (Isaiah 35:10).

Yes, we have reason for hope. But we don't have to wait until we leave this earth to rest in His eternal glory. As we suffer our earthly trials, He doesn't leave us to our own resources. He gave every believer the gift of the Holy Spirit, a mighty Counselor who will never leave us (John 14:16). And when we have the Holy Spirit, we have Jesus himself living inside us (John 14:17). The Holy Spirit teaches us, just like Jesus taught the disciples (John 14:26). He guides us in all our decisions and reveals to us the Father's secrets (John 16:13). He pleads to the Father in our distress (Romans 8:26–27). In the heat of the fire, the Holy Spirit draws us close to the very heart and mind of God.

Jesus talks to us through the Holy Spirit when we stay connected to Him in prayer. He gave us this awesome privilege with His dying breath. In the Old Testament, a curtain hung in the Temple between the Holy Place and the Most Holy Place to prevent anyone from entering God's presence. The curtain represented the separation between a holy and righteous God and a sinful people. Once a year, the high priest was allowed to enter the Most Holy Place and stand in God's presence while he made a blood sacrifice to atone for the sins of the nation (Leviticus 16:1–35; Hebrews 9:1–14). At the moment Jesus died, this sacred dividing curtain was torn in two, and the barrier between God and humanity was removed. Now we can all go boldly into the throne room of God and receive His grace and mercy (Hebrews 4:16). He sacrificed His life to make us pure and holy, worthy of coming into the presence of His Father (Hebrews 10:22). The privilege of prayer was bought and paid for by the blood of Christ. Every time we bow our heads we stand on holy ground.

In those quiet times with Him, we should always have our Bibles open. All Scripture is the inspired Word of God. Through the Holy Spirit, He revealed himself and His plan to certain believers who wrote down His message from their own historical and cultural contexts. They wrote what God told them to write, so when we read His Word, we can know it is trustworthy. The Bible is our standard for testing everything else that claims to be true and our guiding light for how to live. It reveals the true nature of God and the life of abundance we can have in His presence (2 Timothy 3:16–17). There is not one feeling or emotion, from fear and hopelessness to glorious victory, not one situation we will ever encounter, that the sacred Word of God does not address. It speaks to the depths of our suffering and brings comfort in the midst of the deepest sorrow. His Word is full of living power (Hebrews 4:12).

In the fire today, cling tightly to this precious gift and never stop trusting Him (Hebrews 4:14). When all is lost, you have reason for hope. God gave you the free gift of salvation. His Son purchased your freedom on the cross and gave you the glorious promise of eternal life. He gave you the Holy Spirit. He knows your every thought, your every hurt, and your secret longings. Even when you're too heartbroken to pray, the Holy Spirit pleads for you in harmony with God's own will (Romans 8:26–27). He gave you direct access to the Father through the privilege of prayer. You can go boldly into His presence and ask for help when you need it. If you believe, you will receive whatever you ask for (Hebrews 4:16; Matthew 21:22).

And He gave you His eternal and unfailing Word. Opinions change and the world disappoints, but God's Word is constant. Only in His Word will you find lasting solutions to every problem (Isaiah 40:8). Yes, something amazing happens when He joins you in the fire. At the core of your pain, your heart begins to flood with gratitude because God gave you an indescribable gift. He gave you Jesus. Thank God for His Son—a gift too wonderful for words!

Heavenly Father, sometimes I'm so focused on my loss that I miss you in the fire. Thank you for your grace that carries me through each new day. Thank you for the gift of your Son and your promise of eternal life. Thank you for your Holy Spirit that comforts me in my dis-

tress and knows my every need. Lord, I treasure my quiet times with you. I know the privilege of coming into your presence was bought and paid for by your blood. Thank you for your Word that stands the test of time and guides me into all truth. Lord, when all is lost, thank you for hope. You are a gift too wonderful for words! In Jesus' name, amen.

NEVER GIVE UP
THE ENDURANCE TEST

Patient endurance is what you need now, so you will continue to do God's will. Then you will receive all that he has promised.

—HEBREWS 10:36

THE SECRET PATH

Then Jesus said, "Come to me, all of you who are weary and carry heavy burdens, and I will give you rest."

—MATTHEW 11:28

Carol readjusts the cap covering her bald head and fidgets in her chair. It would soon be her turn to give an update. She listens as a young woman with a recent breast cancer diagnosis tearfully shares her story. She thinks about her own first night. How long had she been coming to the prayer meeting? It must be almost two years by now. It seems like forever. She's back in treatment again. Life is an emotional roller coaster. Doctors discover cancer in her liver and tell her to set her affairs in order. She refuses and finds different doctors. She receives several rounds of chemo and the tumors shrink. Praise God! Time passes. Another checkup shows the tumors are growing again. She receives more chemo, but this time, no response. She receives a different chemo and the tumors shrink. Side effects from the chemo land her in the local hospital, but for now, things look good. Until the next checkup. The tumors are growing again. She receives more chemo. Another trip to the hospital. Again she waits, daring to hope. Three months later, scans show spots in two more organs. More tests, more waiting. Never mind, the lesions are benign—a sigh of relief and another glimpse of hope. But soon, tests show new tumors growing in the liver. She receives more chemo. The cycle repeats. Over and over, the cycle repeats. As she updates the group on her latest rounds of tests and treatment, there is deep weariness in her soul. She wonders if it will ever end. Will life ever return to normal, or is *this* the new normal? What will the future bring? She's not sure she can go one more day, let alone the rest of her life.

Howie carefully tucks the latest rejection letter in the file with the job description, company information, and interview notes. He tosses it on top of the growing stack of files. A year ago, when the bottom fell out of his life, he vowed to replace the senior-level job he lost. He made job hunting his full-time job. Now the stack is over a foot high. He's a registered user of every job search Web site on the Internet, and he networks regularly with fellow job seekers. He cold-calls target companies and follows up on every lead. He's applied for hundreds of positions and starts a file on the best opportunities. He's had many interviews. He's even been a finalist several times for positions outside his industry. He's sure this one would have been the perfect fit. His eyes gaze down at the stack on the floor. He's tired of diligently following each opportunity only to reach a dead end. He's tired of the waiting, tired of the emotional highs and lows, and tired of the process. He wonders if he can keep going. Will he ever work again?

There is a weariness deep in our souls that comes from carrying a heavy burden or living through an extended crisis. It goes beyond the physical fatigue that we can cure with a good night's rest or a weekend getaway. The only rest for long-term emotional exhaustion is supernatural. When the flames consume us and we feel we can't go one more step, God offers a secret path to restoration. Jesus experienced it during His earthly ministry. Large crowds seeking hope and healing followed Him everywhere. He faced constant opposition from His enemies as they secretly plotted His murder. He rarely had time alone and often prayed throughout the night (Mark 3:7–12, 6:46–47, 14:1–2). But He never wearied. He knew the secret. His Father restored His soul and gave Him strength.

Only Jesus can give us rest when our weary souls need refreshing. When we're too emotionally exhausted to take another step, we're quick to cry out to Him. *Oh, Lord, I'm so weary! Please give me your rest!* And then we go immediately back to our busy schedule and the business of trying to survive the fire. The Lord *wants* to give us rest. He gives power to those who are tired and worn. He will fulfill His promise to lift us up on wings like eagles' wings, high above the most difficult crisis. But the Lord said those who *wait* on Him would find new strength (Isaiah 40:29–31).

That's right. We need to wait on the Lord and give Him our complete and undivided attention. Part of His process of restoration is to get us to slow down and listen to Him. We may need to take an entire day to just sit in His presence, read His Word, pray, and listen to His voice. In that quiet place, Carol and Howie discovered the secret path. In that quiet place in the presence of Jesus, He can reveal His will. He can show you the solution to a problem you've been trying to fix on your own power. He gives you His peace. He gives you rest for your weary soul.

Is there heaviness in your soul today? Perhaps the fire rages on and on, with no end in sight. Emotionally, you're exhausted. You can barely take another step. You're tired of fighting and your soul thirsts for refreshment. You hear His voice through the fire: *Come to me and I will give you rest.* When you hear His call, you sit at His feet. You give the Savior your undivided attention. He takes you to a place of refreshing green meadows. You soak in His unfailing love, and your soul bathes in His healing waters. You experience His ultimate rest—a peace found only in His presence that is not of this world (John 14:27). You've discovered the secret path to restoration—an intimate relationship with Jesus Christ. Come. Let Him bring rest to your weary soul.

Heavenly Father, I can't take another step. My soul is weary and longs for refreshment. Thank you for your secret path of restoration. Thank you for your unfailing love, your healing power, and the peace of your presence. Lord, help me to wait on you. Show me how to carve out time in my busy day just to sit at your feet and hear your voice. Only you can give me strength to face tomorrow. Please give me a fresh infilling of your Holy Spirit. Let me soak in your love and feel the rejuvenating power of your presence. In Jesus' name, amen.

THE SOUNDS OF SILENCE

Be silent, and know that I am God! I will be honored by every

nation. I will be honored throughout the world.

—PSALM 46:10

The pain was excruciating. Joe had been doctoring for several months, seeking relief for his nagging back pain. He had tried specialists, chiropractors, and massage therapists. He had tried pain-killers, muscle relaxants, and, of course, prayer. Lots and lots of prayer. After all, he was a prayer minister at his church. He had prayed for hundreds of people in worse shape than he was—people with cancer and other life-threatening diseases; people who had lost their jobs or businesses and were in deep financial trouble; people who had kids in jail, cheating spouses, and broken marriages; people with addictions; people in pain. And now he was one of them, and the pain was worse than ever.

A week ago, he bent over to move some boxes. Something snapped in his fragile back. The doctor ordered bed rest. It wasn't too difficult to keep the order, since he couldn't move without coming to tears. He couldn't sleep. He couldn't find any comfortable position. The pain medication made him sick to his stomach. Friends and family gathered around him in prayer. They prayed for a good night's rest; they prayed for pain relief; they prayed for supernatural healing. He wanted to get back to work and back to the business of living. He wanted to avoid a risky surgery and a lengthy rehabilitation regimen at all costs. He wanted a miracle, but God gave him *silence*.

There are times in our walk with Jesus when we find ourselves in a place of silent waiting—waiting for healing to come, waiting to learn the fate of a loved one, waiting for good news while fearing the worst, waiting for a miracle. When we are in this place of waiting, there is nothing we can do in our own power to move the situation forward. Like a helpless little bird, we desperately flap our wings, but nothing happens. Try as we might, we can't take off. We can't move. We can't make God move. Our inner voice screams "Do something!" into the stillness. But God is silent.

When their brother Lazarus became very sick, Mary and Martha sent an urgent message to Jesus. They knew He could heal their brother because they had witnessed His miracle-working power. Jesus loved this family from Bethany. When He heard they needed Him, He waited two full days before responding to their cries for help. He had a bigger plan. He told the disciples that Lazarus's sickness would not end in death, and God would receive glory for what He was about to do. During these two agonizing days of silence, Mary and Martha watched their brother die.

When Jesus finally arrived, Martha said to Jesus, "Lord, if you had been here, my brother would not have died. But even now I know that God will give you whatever you ask"(John 11:21–22). Jesus assured her that Lazarus would rise again. When Jesus saw Mary and the others weeping and wailing over his death, He was moved with compassion and indignation, weeping with them in their sorrow. But He also grieved over their hopelessness when *they had every reason for hope*. The Son of God stood right in the middle of their pain! And indeed, He had a bigger plan. Jesus prayed and called Lazarus out of the tomb. He raised him from the dead to give glory to the Father. All those around Him witnessed the power and sovereignty of Almighty God. But first, there was a time of silence (John 11:1–44).

God's silence always has a specific purpose. His delays might make us think He doesn't hear, He isn't answering our prayers, or He's not answering the way we would like Him to answer. Mary and Martha mourned the silence, just as we often do. But in His silence, God trusted them with a far greater revelation—that their prayer would be used to glorify the Father. If we believe in our hearts that God always hears and always answers our prayers—if we believe He will never give us a snake when we ask for a fish—His silence can be a cause for joy, not despair. It proves that God has heard our cries and has made us part of His sovereign plan—just as He did with Lazarus. In His perfect time He will meet our needs according to His divine purpose (Matthew 7:7–9; Philippians 4:19).

Joe received his healing. God sent him a skilled surgeon, a good physical therapist, and several months of rest. The Lord raised him from the fire, but not before he reached a place of deep humility and a new understanding of his total dependence on God. In the process he gained an even deeper level of compassion for the hurting people he ministered to, and he experienced the beauty of God's grace, the power of His presence, the strength to endure, and growth of his character for God's purposes (James 1:3–4). But not before a time of silence did a mighty work in him!

Today, you too may find yourself in a place of silence. You watch the world around you continue to spin and the people come and go, but your world doesn't move. God has built a wall of fire around you, and there is nothing inside but stillness and waiting. Listen . . . can you hear Him calling? *Take heart, my child. I have overcome your pain and suffering* (John 16:33). *Draw on my unlimited resources and I'll give you strength to endure the heat* (Ephesians 3:16). *My power is mighty and my timing is perfect* (1 Peter 5:6). He wants you to know when the stool collapses underneath you—when the world strips everything away and only the sounds of silence remain—you still have God. And He's orchestrating the perfect plan to bring glory to His Father. You are privileged to be a part of what He's about to do! Be silent, and know that He is God.

Heavenly Father, I want so desperately for you to break the silence! I'm sorry for doubting your sovereign purpose and for pushing ahead of your perfect timing. Even in the stillness, I know you have heard my cries for help; you stand with me in the middle of my pain. Thank you for trusting me with your silence. I believe in my heart you always answer my prayers according to your will. Lord, let your answer to my cries for help bring glory and honor to your name. Please give me strength to endure the heat as I wait in silence for your plan to unfold. In Jesus' name, amen.

A New Start

And let us run with endurance the race that God has set before us.
We do this by keeping our eyes on Jesus, on whom our faith
depends from start to finish.

—Hebrews 12:1–2

The Israelites had everything going for them. After all, the Creator of the Universe *chose* them. He brought them out of slavery into the land of milk and honey and promised to exalt them above all the nations in the world. He promised freedom, prosperity, protection, and a future overflowing with blessing. All they had to do was keep their eyes on the Lord and obey His commands (Deuteronomy 28).

Instead, they followed the pagan practices of the surrounding nations and fell into sin. In His mercy, God sent His prophets to warn them. He continually restored them to His favor, only to have them turn away again. They refused to repent of their sin and scoffed at His prophets until the situation was beyond remedy. In the end, Jerusalem fell to the Babylonians. King Nebuchadnezzar and his army killed Judah's young and old, men and women, healthy and sick. They took all the treasures from the Lord's temple and the royal palace and set them on fire. They broke down the walls of Jerusalem, burned all the palaces, and destroyed everything of value. The few who survived were captured and carried off to Babylon (2 Chronicles 36:14–21).

Even while the people lived in exile for seventy years, God didn't abandon them. As they grieved over their loss and suffered in captivity, He sent a letter of hope and encouragement through the prophet Jeremiah. He instructed them to build homes, plant gardens, marry, and multiply. He told them to move forward with their lives and to pray peace and prosperity over the Babylonian nation that enslaved them. And then He promised to bring them home again. He would give them a future and a hope and listen to their prayers. If they looked for Him earnestly, He promised they would find Him. He would end their captivity and restore their fortunes (Jeremiah 29:5–7, 10–14). Just as He promised, He brought them back to their homeland with renewed hearts for God.

In the fire of oppression, it can be difficult to look forward to a hopeful future. We wallow in our past and lament the things that should have been. We blame our past situations for our present problems. We may be haunted by a difficult home life, past abuse, or deep hurts. Instead of moving forward, our past regrets, current crisis, and a future of uncertainty hold us back. But like the exiles in Babylon, God gave us a promise of hope—He gave us Jesus. We have a brand-new life in Christ! He overcame our past and tossed every mistake into the sea of forgetfulness (Psalm 103:12; Hebrews 8:12). Our old life is gone and new life has come (2 Corinthians 5:17). We are no longer held captive to the sins of the past. We are no longer bound to the ways of the world. By His blood, He freed us from our Babylon.

The world tries to convince us that hope is dead and the past still matters. Jane married at a young age. She and her husband decided to start a family, but midway through the pregnancy he changed his mind and left her. Abandoned and alone, she gave birth to a beautiful baby boy. She struggled to make ends meet as a single mom on a meager income, but even in the darkest times she held on to hope.

Eventually, Jane married a kind and caring man who adored her. He adopted her son and loved him as his own. They had other children and raised a family together. Her son never met his birth father. Through the years they arranged meetings, but his father never came. When news came that he had died from a life plagued with addiction, conflicting and unresolved emotions rose up from deep inside and overflowed into her heart—a broken heart for her son and a relationship that might have been, repentance over her own sin, relief over the lifestyle they escaped, compassion for the broken man who had once been her husband. A lifetime of memories flooded her mind. Through the good times and the bad, she always had Jesus. He had faithfully given her strength to press on. He healed her broken heart. He was her Savior. He had pulled her out of Babylon and given her a future filled with hope.

As Christians, the apostle Paul tells us to focus on what we are becoming, not what we have been. He encourages us to forget the things of the past and move forward to what lies ahead. Paul had reason to forget. Before Jesus won his heart on the road to Damascus, he persecuted Christians relentlessly. Paul had personal knowledge of the depth of God's grace and mercy. He let nothing take his eyes off the goal of knowing Christ personally. He compared his efforts to an athlete in training and let nothing distract him from growing in his relationship with Jesus (Philippians 3:12–14). He encourages us to run the race of life with endurance. Just like Jane, we do this by fixing our eyes on Jesus from start to finish— drawing on His strength and the promise of redemption.

Do past regrets and a hopeless future hold you captive in the fire? The Lord didn't forget you in Babylon. He wants to set you free! He loves you and wants a personal relationship with you. He wants to toss your past mistakes into the sea of forgetfulness. He wants you to know He will right every wrong and avenge every injustice committed against you. He wants to give you a fresh new start. Through the power of the Holy Spirit, He wants to transform your life. So let go of your past and your difficult circumstances. Look forward to what you are becoming! He has plans for good and not for disaster in your life (Jeremiah 31:10–14). Turn to Him in prayer, and He will listen. Seek Him with all your heart, and you will find Him. You have a future filled with hope and you don't have to run the race alone. Keep your eyes on Jesus from start to finish.

Heavenly Father, forgive me for focusing on my past mistakes and my current crisis instead of the future I have in you. Thank you for your compassion and mercy, and for the hope I have in your Son. Thank you for the transforming power of the Holy Spirit. Lord, set me free. Bring me out of my Babylon and give me a fresh new start. Help me to keep my eyes focused on you and what I am becoming. Let nothing distract me from seeking you with all my heart, like an athlete in training. Please give me strength to endure while I look forward with confidence to the promise of my future. In Jesus' name, amen.

READY FOR ANYTHING

For when your faith is tested, your endurance has a chance to grow. So let it grow, for when your endurance is fully developed, you will be strong in character and ready for anything.

—JAMES 1:3–4

The tears stream down Pam's face. A nurse from the clinic called that morning with bad news. The cancer was back. Two years ago, the diagnosis of aggressive breast cancer took her through a difficult journey—a double mastectomy, months of chemotherapy, working through treatment while caring for young children, and coping with the fear of an uncertain future. After treatment ended, each passing month brought healing and hope that the cancer was behind her and her life had been restored. And now it was back, more aggressively than ever. More tests would confirm the extent of metastasis, but statistically, she knows her prognosis just took a turn for the worse. She wipes her tears and makes some phone calls. She arranges to meet a prayer minister later in the day. And then she goes to work.

Jim was an executive vice-president for a Fortune 500 company when he became a casualty of downsizing. For three full years he searched diligently for a job. He followed the latest job search and outplacement strategies to a tee. He didn't need to be an executive—any reasonable job with health benefits would do.

Finally, he took a position at one-third of his former compensation. It didn't matter. He was working again, and his family needed him to work. A few months had passed when he realized the company who had hired him was following some unsavory business practices. They expected him to participate. Instead, he drew a deep breath and jumped back into the fire. Another year passed, and still no job. He continues to look. He continues to trust God's timing and provision.

Marilyn sips her morning coffee and gazes at the rays of sun streaming in the window. It's her first morning alone since the funeral. She opens her Bible and begins to read the familiar passages. She lets God's promises of hope and strength bring comfort to her broken heart. She ponders the notes she made in the margins. She had been to these pages many times before. Nine months earlier, her beloved teenage son had died in a freak accident. Now it was her husband. A sudden heart attack took his life at the early age of forty-seven. She thinks about the life they planned together. She thinks about the unexpected twists and turns, her shattered dreams. As she sips her coffee and turns the page, a peace flows through her—a peace not of this world.

We all know people like Pam, Jim, and Marilyn. Perhaps you know them personally. Or maybe your friends know them, and you stand back and watch them from a distance. We struggle to get our minds around how they cope—how they get themselves out of bed in the morning, go to work and live through the relatively insignificant events filling a typical day, and function through the excruciating pain they must be feeling. Maybe all this wondering took place before the fire. Maybe now you're *one of them*.

Now you understand the invisible line they crossed. There is a sacred place with God, and no one wants to go there. We don't venture there by choice until we face severe testing. Then we go because we have no place else to go. In this sacred place, at the foot of the cross, only Jesus can ease our pain and comfort our souls. Only He knows the depths of our suffering. He's been there. By suffering a violent, bloody death in the hands of His enemies, He shared our human experience and became like us. He feels our pain and cries our tears. He suffered out of perfect love for us (Hebrews 2:9–10). Now, through our own suffering, we are becoming more like Him (Matthew 5:48). Our character is slowly growing in maturity, wholeness, and love toward others (1 John 3:23). And because we share in His suffering, we also share in His victory (1 Peter 5:10).

Sweet victory. As believers, we have a glorious eternal future with Jesus. But until then, we must learn to overcome. Our earthly experience will include trials and hardships that cause our faith to grow. Paul said we should rejoice in our trials because they are good for us (Romans 5:3). James called our trials opportunities for *joy* (James 1:2). I'm sure Pam, Jim, and Marilyn didn't feel any joy. You probably don't either. But it's not our pain that causes us to rejoice. *We rejoice in God's grace in the midst of our sorrow.*

If we yield to Him, He will use the fires of oppression to develop our endurance. Endurance develops strong character and deepens our faith. Through it we gain a confident expectation that we will receive all He has promised (Romans 5:3–4). There is a deep level of dependence and trust in Jesus that we only learn when He is all we have. That inner peace and Christ-like maturity we see in people going through severe testing comes from meeting God in the fire and drawing on His strength to carry us through. The endurance we develop comes from His power, not our own.

When the fire burns on and there is no end to our suffering, endurance deepens our faith. Faith paves the way for God to step in and take control of our problems. But patience keeps the path clear until the results we wait for are evident. Patience comes from strong character and gives our faith a chance to work. Paul encourages us not to throw away our confident trust in the Lord, no matter what happens. He reminds us of the great reward that comes from patient endurance. When our patience is tested and the victory is slow in coming, it's difficult to stay focused on the promises of God. But God promises if we submit to His timing, endure with patience, and continue to obey Him, we will receive our reward. He promises we will not be disappointed (Romans 5:5; Hebrews 10:35–36).

Perhaps you've crossed that invisible line and have met Jesus in that place of deep suffering. We never know the depth of our character until we find ourselves in that sacred place. Don't be discouraged and lose confidence in the Lord, no matter what happens or how long it takes. He won't leave you there longer than necessary. He knows the best time to reach into the fire and change your circumstances (Hebrews 10:35–37). Think about all He endured so that you don't become weary and give up (Hebrews 3:12). The God of all creation—the God who made you—promised He would never fail you (1 Peter 4:19). If He can command the forces of nature, He can certainly see you through your fiery trials. Tell Him what you need and ask Him for the strength to endure. Then patiently wait for all He has promised. Let the power of Jesus grow your endurance. When your endurance is fully developed, you will be strong in character and ready for anything else the world throws at you.

Heavenly Father, today I come to that sacred place at the foot of the cross. I have no place else to go. In this place I share in your suffering, but I also share in your sweet victory. Thank you for loving me so much that you suffered for me. Thank you for crying my tears and feeling my pain. Lord, help me yield to you in the sacred place of my suffering. By your power, let my endurance grow. Strengthen my char-

acter and deepen my faith. Give me patience to wait for your perfect timing. I rejoice in your grace during this time of testing. Let your strength comfort and carry me. Help me become just like you. In Jesus' name, amen.

WELL DONE

The master said, "Well done, my good and faithful servant."

—MATTHEW 25:23

I have a beautiful picture on the background of my computer monitor. My husband took it on the top of Opabin Prospect at Yoho National Park in southeastern British Columbia. I'm standing on the plateau with my arms raised to the heavens and praising the Lord. It's never easy reaching the overlook. It may be a cakewalk for seasoned hikers, but for those who venture into the hiker's heaven of Yoho only once a year, it's a tough climb.

We left our secluded little cabin on the shores of Lake O'Hara surrounded by a spectacular range of snow-covered mountains and hiked our way to the trailhead. Although the weather and the trail conditions can be treacherous and unpredictable, it was a perfect day. As the elevation steadily increased, we hiked carefully through slippery snow-covered rocks and narrow trails. Whenever I needed rest, I found a convenient rock or a fallen tree to sit on and catch a glimpse through the trees of the glorious reward waiting for us at the top.

The first time I hiked this trail, I remember feeling panicked and trapped by the rugged conditions and my own lack of preparation. As I struggled for breath, I couldn't keep going and there was no turning back. This time, however, I looked down at the steep, treacherous trail we had just climbed with a deep sense of satisfaction. I took a gulp of water and kept on climbing. The reward when we reached our final destination was worth every sore muscle at the end of the day—breathtaking panoramic views of glacier-clad peaks touching the heavens and the crystal blue waters of Mary Lake and Lake O'Hara in the valley below.

Every year we hike this trail I feel the same exhilaration when I reach the plateau. It's somewhat like the feeling I have when I complete a manuscript or a difficult project or achieve a lifelong goal. Maybe it gives me a tiny glimpse of how it will feel someday when I meet the Lord face-to-face and He says, "Well done, my good and faithful servant" (Matthew 25:21). This time was extra special. I had just completed several months of chemotherapy. I was praising God for more than His beautiful creation; I was praising Him for delivering me from the fire. I felt like Moses coming down from the mountain that day. My face was glowing. I'd been with Jesus.

Unfortunately, life is not full of mountaintops. There are deep valleys we must walk through—the valley of sickness, the valley of brokenness, the valley of suffering, and the valley of death. How you respond in the valleys will make all the difference in your future, both on this earth and in eternity. The fire burned hot in the valley of suffering that night Jesus was betrayed. When the apostles finally understood that Jesus would not reign over an earthly kingdom, they scattered. When Jesus told them during their last meal together that one of His own disciples would betray Him, they were surprised and confused. That same night, Peter denied Him three times. Only John joined the women at the crucifixion (Matthew 26:31, 56). His own followers didn't want to be identified with Jesus. They feared for their lives and fled. I imagine Jesus was more wounded by the doubt and betrayal of His friends than He was by the cruel and brutal treatment He received from His enemies.

Will you be faithful to Jesus when everyone and everything else in your fire stands against Him? Will you fight the good fight and finish the race? Paul compares his faith journey to a disciplined athlete who trains hard, follows the rules, and is willing to sacrifice to achieve his goal (2 Timothy 4:7). Paul was faithful to his call through a lifetime of persecution. He faced death calmly, confident of the prize at the end of the race. I can compare the race of faith to my hike up that steep mountain trail. We keep going, despite our suffering, because of the prize waiting at the top. Once in a while God encourages us by giving us rest and a little glimpse of our reward through the trees. Whether we walk through the valleys of discouragement, persecution, or death along the way, our reward is a crown of righteousness with Christ in heaven. When we reach the top, God is glorified and we will be able to see that all the pain and suffering we've undergone has been worthwhile. This heavenly reward is for all of us who call Jesus our Lord and Savior and finish the race of faith (2 Timothy 4:8; Hebrews 11:40).

What's the view like on the top of the mountain? Peter asked Jesus a very direct question: "We've given up everything to follow you. What will we get out of it?"(Matthew 19:27). Jesus assured him, and us, that anyone who gives up something valuable for His sake would be repaid many times over in this life (Matthew 19:28). As believers, our earthly reward is God's presence and power through the Holy Spirit. Until we join Him in heaven, the Holy Spirit comforts and guides us, giving us strength to endure our suffering.

When we meet Jesus in the middle of the fire and personally experience His grace and mercy—when we stand on that mountaintop with our arms raised to the heavens—we discover that one single day in His presence is better than a thousand days anywhere else (Psalm 84:10). Knowing we will live forever with God in a place without sin and suffering helps us live above the pain and gives us strength and hope to press on through the darkest valleys. It reminds us that our present troubles are quite small and won't last very long. We look forward to what we haven't seen and the promise of everlasting joy (2 Corinthians 4:17–18). No eye has seen and no ear has heard all God has in store for us in this life or in eternity (1 Corinthians 2:9)!

Right now, a dark cloud may have settled over your valley of suffering. You can't even see the mountain, let alone climb it. Will you desert Jesus when the times get tough, or will you fight the good fight? Can you stay as faithful to Jesus as He is to you? He isn't a drugstore Savior that dispenses quick solutions to your current crisis, only to be forgotten on the shelf until the next time you cry for help. He's a full-time God. He's hiking alongside you up that steep and treacherous mountain trail. His power gives you strength to endure every step as you strain to reach the prize at the top.

He wants the same unwavering devotion from you (Hebrews 13:8). Take a firm stand and don't turn back from the assurance you received when you first heard the Good News (Colossians 1:23). Train hard, obey God with courage, and be ready to sacrifice for what you believe (1 Timothy 6:12). Don't let a day pass without reading His Word, seeking His face, and lifting your hands to the heavens in prayer. Ask the Holy Spirit for endurance to finish the race and remain faithful to the Lord. Then behold His glory when you reach the mountaintop and hear Him say, "Well done, my good and faithful servant. Well done!"

Heavenly Father, forgive me for deserting you when times get tough. Forgive me for letting the distractions of this world take my eyes off of my final destination. Thank you for the promise of eternal life, and for the precious gift of your Son, my ultimate reward. Thank you for your grace and mercy. Lord, every time I stand in your presence, I stand on the mountaintop! Thank you for the Holy Spirit and for giving me

*little glimpses of heaven along the way. Lord, please give me your
strength as I hike through the valley of suffering. Give me endurance to
fight the good fight and finish the race. I want to be your faithful servant. I want to hear you say, "Well done." In Jesus' name, amen.*

BE A BLESSING
THE KINDNESS TEST

He comforts us in all our troubles so that we can comfort others.

When others are troubled, we will be able to give them

the same comfort God has given us.

—2 CORINTHIANS 1:4

FRUIT IN ALL SEASONS

They are like trees planted along the riverbank,

bearing fruit each season without fail. Their leaves never wither,

and in all they do, they prosper.

—PSALM 1:3

Mel is a prayer warrior and a faithful member of the prayer team at his church. Over the years, he's volunteered hundreds of hours ministering to sick and hurting people. Mel is also battling cancer. He's been fighting it for years. From time to time, the cancer comes out of remission and he needs to endure more treatments. Mel keeps right on praying and serving others—chemo or not.

Susan escaped from an abusive marriage. She looks forward to finishing nursing school so she can make a decent living to support her two young children. Her part-time job and financial assistance barely cover their basic needs. The community outreach ministry at her church is helping her get back on her feet. Every week she volunteers her time, serving free meals and helping other moms cope with the issues of single parenting and reentering the workforce.

John lost his job in a corporate buyout. He's starting a new business and struggling to reinvent himself after twenty years in senior management with the same company. Every week, he meets individually with people who come to the community outreach ministry needing employment. He helps them write resumes, complete applications, and search for job openings in the local papers and on the Internet.

Tammy and her husband had been married only a few short years when her dreams were shattered. Her husband died and left her with a one-year-old son. Instead of raising a family together with the man she loved, she would face an uncertain future raising a child alone who would never know his father. In the midst of her heartbreak, she started a grief recovery ministry at her church to help others cope after the loss of a loved one.

Each of these men and women selflessly minister to others in their community of faith who are suffering similar hardships. There are many more like them—people going through divorce, depression, infertility, miscarriage, addiction, financial ruin, or family crisis, people who invited God into the middle of the fire. They are people who focus on serving others instead of focusing on their own suffering, people filled with the Holy Spirit who want others to know the source of their comfort and hope.

The prophet Jeremiah described people who have made the Lord their hope and confidence and are filled with the spirit of God. He said they are like trees planted along a riverbank, with roots that reach deep into the water. They aren't bothered by the heat or worried by long months of drought. Their leaves stay green, and they go right on producing delicious fruit in spite of their difficulties. He contrasts them to those who try to live a life without God and put all their hope in the things of this world. They are unfruitful, like stunted shrubs in the desert, with no hope for the future. They live in the barren wilderness on the salty flats where no one lives (Jeremiah 17:5–8). Without God in our lives, we are spiritually dry and destitute; we have nothing to draw on when heat and drought come. But when God is in the fire with us, we can draw on His abundant strength, not only for our own needs, but to meet the needs of others. Like a well-watered tree, we have strength to endure the fire, and enough left over to bear fruit for the Lord.

Joseph was fruitful in all the seasons of his life. His brothers sold him into slavery when he was only seventeen years old, and he worked hard to serve God and others as an Egyptian slave and prisoner. He was so diligent in his duties that his master, Potiphar, put him in charge of his entire household and entrusted Joseph with all his business dealings (Genesis 39:4). When he was falsely accused and thrown into prison for making improper advances to his master's wife, Joseph didn't complain about his misfortune and give up hope. The years passed and he was long forgotten as he awaited trial. But once again, he did his very best with each assigned task in prison. His diligence and hard work earned him a promotion to prison administrator (Genesis 39:21–23).

When he was hastily pulled out of the dungeon to appear before the king, his right relationship with God gave him favor. He interpreted Pharaoh's dream about a famine that would destroy the land and gave the ruler a plan to save his people from starvation. Pharaoh could see that Joseph was filled with the spirit of God; he put him in charge over the plan, making him second only to the Pharaoh in ruling Egypt (Genesis 41:28–44). Joseph named his second son Ephraim, meaning *fruitful* in Hebrew, because God made him fruitful in the land of his suffering (Genesis 41:52).

Throughout his thirteen years as an Egyptian slave and prisoner, Joseph's focus was on serving others rather than his own suffering. Everyone he encountered could see the spirit of God in him. In the land of your suffering, do people see God's spirit in you? They will know He dwells in you by your fruit. When the Holy Spirit controls your life, He produces love, joy, peace, patience, kindness, goodness, faithfulness, gentleness, and self-control—character traits found in the nature of Christ (Galatians 5:22–23). You won't produce this fruit in your own power. Just as a tree soaks up water and bears delicious fruit without fail, you can prosper in the land of your suffering because your life is joined with His (John 15:4–5). You know and love Him, and His Word is etched in your heart. Your roots grow down deep into His life-giving water (Isaiah 58:11). In the good times or bad, people come to the riverbank and sit under your shade. You bear fruit in all seasons, and there's plenty left over to share.

Heavenly Father, forgive me for focusing so much on my own pain that I haven't noticed the pain of those around me. Come, Lord Jesus, come into my fire. Fill me with your Holy Spirit. I want to be that tree on the riverbank that prospers in all seasons. Like Joseph, please make me fruitful in the land of my suffering. Let my roots grow down deep into your life-giving water. Let me draw on your strength to endure the fire, and may I have enough left over to produce delicious fruit for you. Let others see your spirit in me. In Jesus' name, amen.

PLANTING IN TEARS

Restore our fortunes, Lord, as streams renew the desert. Those who plant in tears will harvest with shouts of joy. They weep as they go to plant their seed, but they sing as they return with the harvest.

—PSALM 126:4–6

Our motorcycles climbed slowly through the smoky haze covering the Going-to-the-Sun Road in Glacier National Park. The gray smoke filled our nostrils and burned our eyes, and it became more difficult to breathe. As the elevation increased, we were greeted with panoramic views of the valleys below. Thick black clouds of smoke rose from patches of burning forest and filled the horizon. When traveling a few years earlier on this same road, the sheer beauty of glacier-clad peaks plunging into the deep green valleys below had taken my breath away. Images of alpine meadows, thick forests of hemlocks and cedars, and waterfalls cascading over cliffs into pristine blue lakes were planted firmly in my memory. Now as far as the eye could see there was nothing but charred waste-land. I wondered how long it would take before signs of new life would start peeking through the skeletons of burnt trees covering the landscape.

It wasn't the first time I wondered if life could be restored after the fire. A few years earlier, as I stared into my bathroom mirror, a bald woman stared back at me. Her eyes were big and brown, more obvious now that her eyelashes and eyebrows had fallen out along with the rest of her hair. It was a side effect of the chemo. Purple bruises from several failed attempts to insert the IV needle covered the top of her hand and the insides of her wrist and arm. She was halfway through treatment for invasive breast cancer. Weeks had turned to months, and time seemed to stand still.

I remembered how she used to look—long black hair touching her shoulders, her makeup meticulously applied as she got ready for a typical day of meetings, mothering, and the simple tasks of living. What would the future bring? Would she live to see her children get married? Would she ever meet her grandchildren? Would her hair grow back? I studied her eyes and could see into the charred wasteland of her soul. A single tear ran down her cheek. Would her life ever be restored?

Our human tendency is to let despair and self-pity consume us when the tough times come. But the Psalmist says those who plant in tears will harvest with shouts of joy. If we reach out and bless others during this time of weeping, we will receive a fruitful harvest from the seed we plant. I made a choice that day in the dark bald wasteland. Out of the charred coals of the fire came a decision to sow my tears into the hearts of others. I prayed for people receiving chemo at the clinic alongside me. I wrote words of encouragement to people suffering from cancer. I started a prayer ministry at my church for people with cancer and the families who love them. And God was faithful to His promise. He used the seeds I planted to bring new life into the charred wasteland of my soul. He healed my body and restored my life. The harvest continues, and the ministries born out of my suffering bless many. I am privileged to speak and write God's message of hope into the hearts of others in the refining fire.

God's amazing ability to restore life is beyond our limited human understanding. He can restore a beautiful park after a devastating fire. He can restore health after cancer. He can restore broken bodies, broken relationships, broken homes, and broken hearts. He is able to bring good out of tragedy and turn the darkness into light (John 12:46). For hundreds of years, He promised through the prophets to restore His fallen kingdom to its former glory (Amos 9:11). He fulfilled the promise in Christ's resurrection (Acts 15:16–17). Through the gift of redemption, He removed your sin and restored you to himself. You have been declared righteous so you can know Him personally and experience His peace (Romans 4:24–25, 5:1). Yes, your God can bring new life from the fire that threatens to destroy you. He can produce a harvest of blessing from the seeds of your pain.

What kind of harvest will God bring from your tears? Right now, your suffering may feel like it will never end. Planting seeds into others may be the last thing on your mind. You may even feel like God has abandoned you in a pile of ashes. Deep inside, your soul may feel barren and lifeless, like a forest after a devastating fire. But God promises that if you don't get discouraged and give up—if you plant seeds that please Him—you will reap a harvest of blessing in due time (Galatians 6:9).

It's not too late. The planting season isn't over. Reach out to a person in need. Invest in someone else who is suffering. Give yourself away in spite of your pain. Ask God how you can be a blessing. Very soon, the charred wasteland of your soul will come to life again. God will bring more blessings from your tears than you can count. You may be weeping as you go out to plant, but you'll be singing for joy when you return with the harvest!

Heavenly Father, forgive me for wallowing in my own self-pity and despair. Thank you for the gift of redemption and for restoring me to yourself through the sacrifice of your Son. Thank you for bringing new life into the charred wasteland of my soul. Lord, show me how I can be a blessing to those who need your promise of hope. Give me the strength and desire to plant in tears. Let there be songs of joy when the harvest comes! In Jesus' name, amen.

REAL LOVE

Dear children, let us stop just saying we love each other;

let us really show it by our actions.

—1 JOHN 3:18

Do you know what real love is? Jesus told the story of a Jewish man who was brutally attacked by thieves while traveling to Jericho. They stripped him of his clothes and money, beat him up, and left him to die beside the road. First a Jewish priest, and then a temple assistant came along. They were both religious leaders, but when they saw the man lying there, they crossed to the other side of the road and passed him by. Then came a despised Samaritan. When he saw the man, he felt deep compassion. He soothed the man's wounds with medicine and bandaged them. Then he put the man on his own donkey and took him to an inn, where he made arrangements for his care at the Samaritan's expense (Luke 10:30–35).

The religious people were *too busy* to minister to someone God had placed in the road in front of them. They had things to do and places to go. Of all people, the Samaritan had plenty of good reasons not to help. The Jews prided themselves in being pure descendents of Abraham. They viewed the Samaritans as a mixed race, produced when the Israelites in the northern kingdom intermarried with people from other nations. The Jews and Samaritans were fierce enemies, so the Samaritan on the road to Jericho probably felt no love for this dying man. But unlike the religious Jews who failed to help their own in need, this man stopped. He was not too busy to show God's grace and mercy to the suffering. He showed real love by his actions.

God expects more from His children than dutiful worship and religious piety. The real evidence of our love for Him is in how we treat other people. Howie was a busy, upstanding businessman. He rarely missed a Sunday service. Before the fire, he wouldn't have noticed Maria and Antonio on the road. Even if he could see how desperate they were, he would have been too busy to stop. His business travel back and forth to Europe and his high-stress job left barely enough time to keep his own spiritual tank filled. He had no time to worry about someone else's. When he lost his job and the stool beneath him crumbled, Jesus met Howie in the fire and changed his life.

Maria and Antonio had escaped from the terror and lawlessness of Colombia. They were struggling to make a new life for their family in America when they met Howie through their pastor. They were frightened, and their needs were great. They had been misinformed, passed by, and exploited at every turn since their arrival. Howie had become quite an expert in finding work and helping others do the same, so he started by helping Maria to find a job. Then he discovered that Antonio was qualified for unemployment assistance, so he helped him file the paper work and carefully explained to him the complicated process for collecting.

When he visited their home, he found them carrying buckets of water from the shower to the kitchen sink. So he quickly found a plumber willing to donate his time to repair the broken kitchen faucet. He discovered the roof leaked also, so he brought a friend over to help him fix it. Howie learned that their car was undependable and the heater was broken—they had to use a blanket to keep warm in the cold Minnesota winter—so he arranged for repairs. Then he realized most of their limited income went to pay the 19 percent interest on their trailer home and for the heat that escaped through its leaky windows. He spent weeks tracking down the title so Maria and Antonio could sell it and find comfortable housing.

Howie took time to stop on the road and soothe the wounds of this hurting family. As he mentored them through employment issues, immigration paper work, car problems, insurance issues, school concerns, landlord negotiations, and property purchases, he came to love and care for them deeply. Now they own their own home. Their oldest son is in college. They both work and bless others in their church through the translation services and help they provide to families facing language and cultural barriers. Because Howie met Jesus in his fire, Maria and Antonio met Him in theirs. Howie showed real love, and many were blessed by his actions.

But he was himself blessed too. When he submitted to Christ and let Him reign in his life, his heart slowly softened. The kindness and comfort of Jesus naturally started to overflow to those around him. When we invite God into the fire and the Holy Spirit comes to live inside us, He slowly makes us more like Christ.

Like Howie, we all receive a personal invitation to let Jesus carry out His work in our lives. If we accept it, we become His hands and feet. We show real, selfless love for others through our actions, just like Jesus showed toward us. We bring kindness, charity, and generosity with us wherever we go. We serve others without expecting anything in return. We love like Jesus loves, and we are richly blessed. If God's perfect love is truly within us, how can we ignore a brother or sister in need (1 John 3:16–17)? As Christ followers, nothing should stand in the way when the clear voice of God invites us to stop on the road and join Him in the work of His kingdom.

The people God places in front of you are no accident; He has prepared these *divine appointments* especially for you. He knows what they need, and He has a given you the exact resources you need to help them. He wants to accomplish great things in their lives through you. Don't miss out on His sacred call. It's not just for you that His peace brings you comfort during these times of great sorrow. It's not just for you that He miraculously provided for your needs and rescued you from the fire. He has carefully prepared your heart to bear the burdens of others (Galatians 6:2). You know exactly how they feel. You know every fear, every pain, and every emotion. As He has comforted you, let your comfort overflow to those around you (2 Corinthians 1:3–4). Show some real love today.

Heavenly Father, forgive me for the times I've ignored your call to help someone in need. Thank you for sending the Holy Spirit to live inside me and make me more like your Son. Lord, I accept the sacred invitation to join you in your kingdom's work. Thank you for the divine appointments you are preparing just for me! Please give me a heart filled with real, selfless love for others. Help me hear your voice through the fire when you call me to stop on the road. Let your kindness and comfort overflow to those around me. Let me show real love; help me be your hands and feet. In Jesus' name, amen.

LET THE RIVERS FLOW

"If anyone thirsts, let him come to Me and drink.

He who believes in Me, as the Scripture has said,

out of his heart will flow rivers of living water."

—JOHN 7:37–38 (NKJV)

When Jesus first sent the Holy Spirit to His followers, it was no small thing. It was nothing short of spectacular. It happened on the day of Pentecost, seven weeks after Jesus' resurrection. Suddenly, a roaring sound like a mighty windstorm came down from heaven and filled the house where the believers were meeting. When flames of fire appeared and settled on each of them, they were filled with the Holy Spirit and began speaking in other languages. Godly Jews from many nations came running when they heard the sound and were confused to hear their own languages being spoken by the believers. Many in the crowd were convinced they were drunk, even though it was only nine o'clock in the morning (Acts 2:1–5, 13–15)!

When the Holy Spirit comes to the modern-day believer, it is no small thing either. The Spirit comes to you and me and all who accept Jesus as Savior (John 14:16–17). When we receive the Holy Spirit, we receive the gift of eternal life, a gift that only Jesus can give (John 3:16). From the moment we first believe He is Lord, the Holy Spirit comes to live in us and empower us. The old self is dead and eternity begins. We have God's supernatural, resurrection power within us—our own personal Savior (Romans 8:9–11).

Do you realize the sheer magnitude of that power? The spirit of the living Christ dwells in our hearts. The Spirit of God, the same God that held the oceans in His hand, measured off the heavens with His fingers, and knows the weight of the earth, the One who created all the stars, calls them each out by name, and counts them to make sure none are lost (Isaiah 40:12, 26)—this Spirit is within us! Now, *that's* serious power. No wonder the heavens roared and tongues of fire descended when His Spirit came to ignite the hearts of His people!

It only makes sense that if the Holy Spirit lives inside us and we submit to His power, big things will happen. *Really* big things, nothing-short-of-spectacular things, are possible. Jesus said when the Holy Spirit lives in us, rivers of living water would flow out of our hearts to those around us. Think of it . . . when we are dry and parched, we go to Christ and drink from His perpetual spring of living water to refresh our thirsty souls (John 4:14). Then, when we have been fully satisfied, His living water flows out from our hearts to bless the hearts of others—not just down the hall to a family member or co-worker, or down the street to a neighbor in need, but to the very ends of the earth (Acts 1:8)!

As the living waters flow out of our hearts, we may never know how far the river flows beyond us. We may never see the people we touch or the blessings that come from the Holy Spirit dwelling inside us. Only the Father knows the impact that our decision to believe in the Son will have on His kingdom (John 6:29). Think of it this way. Howie reaches into the fire of an unemployed father named Bill and shows him the love of Christ. He prays with him, encourages him, and coaches him through the job search process. Bill meets Jesus in the fire, and his life is changed. Eventually, he starts a seekers' Bible study over the noon hour at his new job. He begins to minister and pray with Ann, a co-worker struggling with a troubled teen. As a result, Ann seeks help for her son through a Christian residential program for chemically dependent teens. Her son graduates from the program and starts a street ministry for drug-addicted teens that eventually expands to other large cities. Soon thousands of teens are set free from drugs and receive Jesus as Lord. And the rivers flow on.

Now, *that's* power. The rivers flow out of Howie's heart down a far-reaching path, bringing living water to many thirsty souls. He doesn't need a "receipt" for the work God accomplishes through his one single act of love. He will never know how far the river flows or how many people will be blessed by his obedience. He stands on the promise that God's Word *never* comes back empty. God sends out His Word, and it always produces fruit; it accomplishes all He wants to accomplish and it prospers everywhere He sends it (Isaiah 55:11). Howie's role is to love and be a blessing to the people, the "divine appointments," God places in his path. When he lets the river flow from his heart, God will handle the rest.

The rivers flow continuously from our hearts, and all is well . . . until an obstacle comes along and blocks the flow. Anything that takes our eyes off the Source—unconfessed sin, fears, emotions, and the everyday stresses in life—can block the flow of living water. Then God can no longer use us as a life-giving channel. Sin offends our holy and righteous God and separates us from our life Source (Isaiah 59:2). But if we turn back to God with a repentant heart, if we go back to our Source of living water, He will restore our relationship with Him and replenish our souls, removing the obstacles in our path or guiding us gently around them. Once we become an unblocked channel, the river can flow through us. All who are thirsty can come and drink.

Today, you may feel more like the Dead Sea than a steady flowing river. Perhaps you've received His life-giving water, but you're keeping it all for yourself in a stagnant holding tank inside your heart. Or perhaps your spirit is so dry that your whole body thirsts in this parched and weary land of your suffering (Psalm 63:1). Maybe it's time to go drink from the well and let Him replenish your soul. If your relationship is right with God, His blessings will flow out from you in the same measure they flow in (Luke 6:38). If you show kindness to others as the Lord has shown kindness to you—if you feed the hungry and help those in trouble—He will guide you continually and water your life when you are dry. You will be like a well-watered garden or an ever-flowing spring (Isaiah 58:7, 10–11).

Don't let anything block the channel. You have the almighty powerful Spirit of God inside you. Let the rivers of blessing run through your heart and reach all the way to the ends of the earth. People you don't even know will come and drink from its living water. Let the rivers flow!

Heavenly Father, forgive me for letting any obstacles come between us that would block the outpouring of your blessing to others. Thank you for the gift of your Spirit and the power of the resurrection that lives inside me. Lord, you are my personal Savior, and my soul is parched and thirsty. I come to drink from the perpetual well of your living water. Please give me a fresh infilling of your Spirit! Lord, I want to be a clear channel for your love to flow through. Show me any unconfessed sin in my heart. Help me focus on you, the Source, and not the obstacles that would block your channel of blessing. Let the rivers of your living water continue to flow from my heart. In Jesus' name, amen.

YOUR LIGHT HAS COME!

Arise, shine; For your light has come!
And the glory of the Lord is risen upon you.

—ISAIAH 60:1 (NKJV)

Today in the fire of oppression, you fall to the ground and worship your God. You cry out to Him from the depths of your pain. The Silversmith meets you in the middle of the fire, and He brings good news: The time of His gracious favor has come! He has come to comfort your broken heart and set you free. He has come to give you beauty for ashes, joy instead of mourning, and hope instead of despair (Isaiah 61:1–3). As He reaches out His nail-pierced hand, you hear His voice in the blazing inferno. *Arise from sickness, sorrow, doubt, and depression! Arise from hunger, poverty, and limitation! Arise from confusion, worry, fear, and brokenness! Arise! Shine! Your light has come! The glory of the Lord is risen upon you!* You stand up and bask in His presence; you have seen the face of God.

Moses fasted and prayed in the presence of God for forty days and forty nights on the top of Mount Sinai. When he came down the mountain, carrying the stone tablets inscribed with the terms of the covenant—the Ten Commandments—his face glowed because he had spoken to the Lord face-to-face. The people of Israel were so afraid when they saw Moses that he had to cover his face with a veil. He removed the veil whenever he went to speak with the Lord, and again, the people would see his face aglow.

They could clearly see God's presence in him (Exodus 34:28–35). They knew God spoke to him face-to-face, as a man speaks to a friend (Exodus 33:11).

If the old covenant began with so much glory that the people could barely look at Moses' face, just imagine the power of the new covenant (2 Corinthians 3:9). The light of the world has come! The sacrifice of Jesus Christ gave us new life through the Holy Spirit. If we follow Him in faith, we will never stumble through the darkness again. We have the light that leads to eternal life (John 8:12). When the apostles brought His light into the world, they performed miraculous signs and wonders among the people. The blind received their sight, the lame walked, demons were cast out, and all were healed (Acts 5:12–16). They presented the news of Jesus Christ with an authority and boldness that amazed the rulers, elders, and teachers of religious law (Acts 4:18–20). The disciples were just ordinary people with no special training. But they had been with Jesus (Acts 4:13).

And so have you. Even *greater* things will you do (John 14:12). God didn't save you for your own benefit. Yes, He loves you. You are His child, and His love for you knows no limits. He proved it when He suffered and died for you. But He didn't give you the gift of salvation for your own purposes. He didn't reach down and rescue you from the fire for your own selfish reasons. You are not your own (1 Corinthians 6:19). Your pain has opened the doorway to the throne room of God. You met Him face-to-face in the fire. If you let Him, He will pour out His love for the world through your broken heart. You have the awesome privilege of joining Him in the work of His kingdom. Working in the power of the Holy Spirit, you can share His love with your family, your friends, your neighbors, your co-workers, and anyone else God sends you to as His witness.

Will you accept His invitation? If your answer is yes, you face a future of unlimited power to bless others. Through the saving grace of Jesus, you are being made perfect for God's purposes. You are becoming just like Him. As you spend more time with Him, in your Bible and in prayer, you begin to light up the darkness around you. With the veil removed, you become a mirror that brightly reflects His character (2 Corinthians 3:18). After all, you've been in the middle of the fire where the flames burn hottest.

The Silversmith never left you there unattended. He protected you from the flames and gave you hope and encouragement to endure the intense heat. Ever so gently, He skimmed off the impurities and left nothing behind but pure holiness. And now, the reflection people see in the purified silver is beginning to resemble the Silversmith. You reflect His glory wherever you go and everyone comes to bask in your glow. You have seen the face of God. He has given you grace for the tough times. Arise, shine! Your light has come!

Heavenly Father, thank you for never leaving me alone through the tests of the fire. Thank you for protecting me from the flames raging around me. Forgive me for the times I resisted you and tried to make it on my own strength. Even then, your grace covered me. Lord, I saw your face in the fire, and my life will never be the same. I will never have to stumble around in the darkness again! As I step out of the furnace and into the world, may I be like a mirror reflecting your character to others. Let everyone see your presence in me. Holy Spirit, please give me courage and boldness to pour out your love and share the source of my hope wherever you send me. Praise God—My light has come! In Jesus' name, amen.